The
Internet
Business
Companion

The Internet Business Companion

Growing Your Business in the Electronic Age

David Angell
Brent Heslop

Addison-Wesley Publishing Company

Reading, Massachusetts • Menlo Park, California
New York • Don Mills, Ontario • Wokingham, England
Amsterdam • Bonn • Sydney • Singapore • Tokyo • Madrid
San Juan • Paris • Seoul • Milan • Mexico City • Taipei

Library of Congress Cataloging-in-Publication Data
Angell, David.
   The Internet business companion : growing your business in the
electronic age / David Angell, Brent Heslop.
    p. cm.
   Includes index.
   ISBN 0-201-40850-3
   1. Business enterprises—United States—Communication systems.
   2. Internet (Computer network)   3. Information networks.
   4. Communication, International.   I. Heslop, Brent D.   II. Title.
   HD30.335.A54   1995
   004.6'7—dc20   94-20331
                                                               CIP

Sponsoring Editor: Philip Sutherland
Project Manager: Sarah Weaver
Technical Reviewer: Andrew Currie
Cover design: Barbara T. Atkinson
Text design: Shepherd, Inc.
Set in 10 point Palatino by Shepherd, Inc.

1 2 3 4 5 6 7 8 9 -MA- 9897969594
First printing, October 1994

Addison-Wesley books are available for bulk purchases by corporations, institutions, and other organizations. For more information please contact the Corporate, Government, and Special Sales Department at (800) 238-9682.

Contents

Contents

❏ ACKNOWLEDGMENTS

We could not have completed our journey through the world of virtual commerce without the help of many talented and helpful people along the way. First and foremost, we want to thank Phil Sutherland at Addison-Wesley for giving us the opportunity to work on this project. Phil was a constant source of ideas and support. Thanks also to Matt Wagner at Waterside Productions for handling the business side of this project.

Many people helped answer questions that we faced as we erected our own business presence on the Internet. Rich White at Portal Communications spent hours, both day and night, helping us with our technical questions. Andrew Currie at Cyberspace Development reviewed our manuscript and helped us with business solutions throughout the project. We also would like to thank Bob Berger at InterNex, Jon Zeff at Branch Information Services, John Groves at The Internet Company, Marc Fleischmann at Internet Distribution Services, Clint Heiden at Intercon, and Jayne Levin at *The Internet Letter,* all of whom freely shared their valuable insights. A special thanks to John Mayes and Johnson Wu of John Mayes & Associates for helping us set up our Sun Workstation, and Mike Koponeck and Jon Blake, at Rockwell International, who proved to be paragons of patience in helping us set up a router.

At the heart of any Internet connection is the service provider; we would like to thank the service providers who provided IP accounts and support services throughout this project. Thanks to Michael Byman at AlterNet; Desirree Madison-Biggs and Rick Francis at NETCOM; John Little, Brian Fudge, and Anju Chowdhry at Portal Communications; and Laurie Johnson, Melissa Parker, Arthur Hyun, John Logalbo, John Becker, and Gary Silber at PSI. Of course, no connection is complete without TCP/IP software. While several companies provided us with TCP/IP software, we used NetManage's Chameleon on the PC for most of our research and want to thank Bob Williams, Donna Loughlin, and Mike Baglietti at NetManage for their support.

Other people and companies (alphabetically by company) that helped us on this project by supplying information, products and services include:

Rebecca Michals at Adobe Systems Inc.
Margaret Ryan at America Online
Scott Stien at Applied Network Comunications
Jerri Emm at Ascend Communications
Rich Siegel at Bare Bones Software
Jaye Day at Beame & Whiteside

Acknowledgments

Brian McGarry at CE Software Inc.
Gina Espejo at Cisco Systems
Scott Estridge at Combinet
Bill Washburn at Commercial Internet Exchange
Chris Hamilton at EI Net
Steve Harari at EIT
Ronald Linehan and Peg Dawson at Electric Press
Laura McKelvy at FARNET
Steve Sollstad at Frontier Technologies
Patrick Pecorelli at FTP Software
George Boyce and Jack Kalser at Global Electronic Marketing Service
Cathy Bower and Doris Naujeck at Global Village
Brent Chapman at Great Circle Associates
Beth McElveen at Hayes
Suzanne Koumantzelis at Holonet
Jon Jackson at Intel
Robert Herzberg at the Internet Business Report
Robert Raisch, Bill Love, and John Groves at The Internet Company
Bill Rollinson at the Internet Shopping Network
Dwain Stone, Ann Cooper, and Gleason Sackman at InterNIC
Dave Taylor at Intuitive Systems
Lisa Rizzo at Ipswitch Inc.
Jim McBride at J.S. McBride & Associates
Wes Walton at Livingston Enterprises
Smoot Carl-Mitchell at Matrix News
Laura Beck at McGlinchey & Paul Public Relations (Lotus Development)
Connie Roloff at McQuerter Group (Public Relations for Qualcomm)
Rona Michele at Michele~Shine Media
Dan Latendre at MKS
Dave Dawson and K. James Laskey at Morning Star Technologies
Barbara J. Brodley at Notis Systems Inc.
Laura Fillmore at Online Bookstore
Greg Marshall and Scott Adams at Pacific Bell
Marianne McCarthy at Rockwell International
Dave Close and Alyson Buckholtz at Shwartz Communications, Inc.
    (SunSelect)
Christopher Mahoney at Software Ventures
Deanna Leung at Spry
Michael Strangelove at Strangelove Enterprises
Michelle Hnath at Synergy Software

Acknowledgments

Maggie Parkinson and Lois Long at Telebit
Gail Williams at the WELL
Stacy Pena Thomas Associates (Public Relations for Farallon)
Lauri Lentz at U.S. Robotics
John During and Ben Lai at WAIS Inc.
Alison Janse at WellFleet
Michael Faklis at West Coast Live
Earle Speranza at Wollongong
Lesa Carter at WordPerfect Corporation
Munira Brooks at Zyxel

Last but not least, our most heartfelt thanks goes to our wives, Joanne Angell
and Kim Merry, who helped us keep our sanity throughout the writing of
this guide.

❑ READ ME FIRST

More than 38 million people are now connected to the Internet, and 100 million people will be connected by 1998. The Internet is the communications and data movement medium that is rapidly defining how business will be done in the future—and the future has arrived. The Internet offers dramatic opportunities to improve business productivity and open up new, untapped markets on a global scale. Savvy businesspeople who set up shop and get accustomed to conducting business in cyberspace today will see their companies grow right along with the exponential growth of the Internet. Even the smallest firm can afford to set up an integrated and impressive presence on the Internet to conduct virtual commerce. However, establishing a business presence on the Internet is a complex process that requires navigating through a myriad of changing, converging, and intertwining technical, financial, and management issues where few options are cut-and-dried.

The Internet Business Companion puts you in the driver's seat as it takes you through the process of establishing a cost-effective Internet business presence. This book doesn't bog you down with unnecessary technical details. It's a practical guide that filters the vast tangle of divergent information and assembles it into an Internet business plan you can work with to manage others—such as service providers, server services, and consultants—to construct your business presence in cyberspace.

The process of establishing an Internet business presence is broken down into three essential parts: getting your business wired to the Internet, setting up a server presence to deliver services online; and working with the key tools of the Internet trade, including e-mail, network news, FTP, Gopher, and World-Wide Web. This guide delivers the information you need to be an educated consumer and to find the right resources for setting up shop on the Internet.

The Internet Business Companion is a snapshot of the available options for establishing an Internet business presence over the time this book was written. Keep in mind that commerce on the Internet is constantly changing. If you have any experiences or discoveries that could be included in future editions of this book, or if you have any comments about this guide, send us e-mail.

David Angell
dangell@bookware.com

Brent Heslop
bheslop@bookware.com

Chapter 1

❑ ❑ ❑

The Internet and Virtual Commerce

In 1991, for the first time in history, U.S. companies spent more on computing and communications equipment than on industrial capital goods. The industrial age has given way to the information age. Computer and communications technology is the new infrastructure of the modern economy. The Internet, which is itself the result of a marriage of global communications and computers, is rapidly becoming the new medium of this information economy. The race is on for *virtual commerce* on the Internet, which is the conducting of business in cyberspace. *Cyberspace* is any virtual world provided by any network of computers, including the Internet. This chapter orients you to the Internet and its commercial opportunities. It explains what the Internet is, how it works, its demographics, its march toward commercialization, and the opportunities the Internet offers businesses.

❑ THE INTERNET: AN EXECUTIVE SUMMARY

Unless you've been living in a cave, you've heard something about the Internet. Despite the constant media coverage of the Internet, most non-users are still confused about what the Internet is. It's helpful to think of the Internet as a vast digital highway system that links millions of computers connected to thousands of networks around the world. While there is no one centralized system of management of the Internet, a hierarchy of networks exists. Backbone networks provide the high-speed and high-volume data links between regional networks. One of the best known backbone networks is the NSFNET, which is funded by the federal government. Other backbones are provided by education and commercial organizations. The backbones deliver data between regional areas to large regional networks, which in turn deliver data to smaller networks. Every connected network site is governed by its own internal operations. Connected via a

1

common communications medium, all these sites make up the Internet. Resources for the operation of the Internet come from each player. In other words, each player maintains its portion of the Internet connection through which information from other networks is routed. Figure 1.1 illustrates the matrix of networks that make up the Internet.

FIGURE 1.1
The Internet is a network of networks

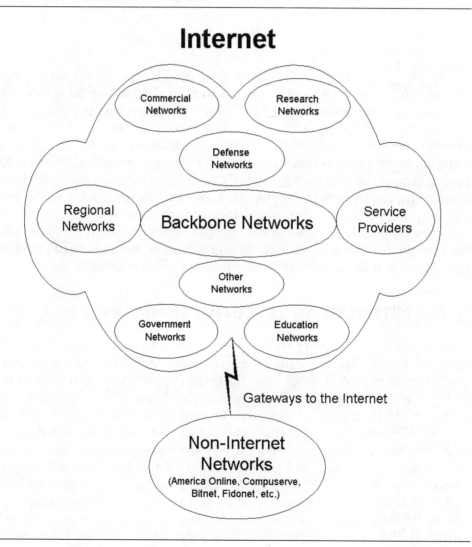

The Internet was born from the R&D (research and development) demands of the military-industrial complex, acting as a research conduit for the government, universities, and large corporations. As the Internet became more popular, commercial organizations began offering access to the Internet so that people who were not researchers could connect to the Internet. As a result, the Internet has become a network of more than 15,000 networks connecting over 38 million people, with an additional 150,000 connecting each month for the first time. By 1998, it's projected that 100 million people will be using the Internet.

Understanding the key concepts behind the Internet will help you throughout the process of establishing your business presence on the Internet. The following sections give you the boiled-down version of how the Internet works and the main tools for working on the Internet.

The TCP/IP Connection

The Internet is the largest network on the planet, with all kinds of different computers connected to it. The computers talk to each other using *protocols*, which are rules or agreements on how to communicate. Think of protocols as a kind of *Robert's Rules of Order* for networking. For two different types of computers to communicate with each other, they have to be using the same protocol.

TCP/IP, which stands for Transmission Control Protocol/Internet Protocol, is the standard protocol of the Internet. It lets all the different computers connected to the Internet communicate with each other. Any computer that wants to communicate with any other computer on the Internet must speak TCP/IP. TCP/IP was developed by DARPA, the early predecessor of the Internet. Because TCP/IP was a nonproprietary protocol (an open protocol not owned by any single organization), it was incorporated into most versions of the UNIX operating system. This marriage of UNIX and TCP/IP is one of the main reasons that the dominant operating system used on the Internet is UNIX. In turn, TCP/IP emerged as the standard communications protocol of the Internet because of its integration with the UNIX operating system. UNIX offers the security and multitasking features demanded by large networks. TCP/IP is now available for other computer operating systems, including DOS and Windows, the Macintosh, and others. Associated with the TCP/IP protocol are some standard TCP/IP applications or tools for performing different tasks, such as sending and receiving electronic mail, transferring files, and accessing files remotely.

How Information Moves across the Internet

The Internet is a communications and data movement medium primarily based on the TCP/IP *packet-switching* networking scheme. A packet-switching network breaks data into small chunks; each chunk is sent across the network in a packet that contains source and destination information. Because each packet has its addressing information built in, it can travel independently. This information allows an enormous number of packets to flow through the network using different routes, yet each reaches its appropriate destination in one piece. The packets may arrive out of order, but because each packet also contains sequence information, the receiving computer can reconstruct the original data. Because it uses this process of transmitting data, the Internet is referred to as a packet-switched network. The switches are computers or other devices called *routers*. Think of routers as being the airport hubs of the Internet. Each router connects several different networks. The router figures out the best routes for the packets to take and shuttles the packets to and from the different networks. The Internet has a network hierarchy of sorts in terms of the transmission of data. The high-speed central networks are known as backbones. The equivalent of the interstate highway system, backbones accept data traffic from and deliver it to the midlevel networks. These midlevel networks, in turn, take the traffic from the backbones and distribute it to networks within their regional area, thus constructing the neighboring roads of the networking world.

Client/Server Foundation of the Internet

Fundamentally any two computers connected via the Internet follow the *client/server* model. A *client* is any computer remotely connected to a host computer, called a *server*, to run programs across the network. Establishing a business presence on the Internet is a combination of client and server activities. Businesses can use client programs to work on other host computers on the Internet. But a business can also establish a server presence to have Internet users connect to its server to get information or conduct business.

You use a *client program* to access a server version of a program running on a host computer on the Internet. Clients and their respective server programs use the same protocol to communicate. The client program provides the user interface for working with the server program. It takes commands you execute from your computer and conveys them to the server program running on the host computer. For example, an Internet user can use the client program Mosaic to connect and work on a World-Wide Web server.

4

Once it is connected to the server computer, the client program receives information from the server program and displays the output on the client's screen as if the server were directly connected to the client's computer.

Internet Addressing

Every computer directly connected to the Internet has its own address, much like a postal address. Knowing the Internet address is as important as knowing postal addresses for sending letters. Two main types of addresses work together on the Internet—*IP addresses* and *domain names*—to make up an *Internet address.* Both IP addresses and domain names are important, and you will be exposed to them in many areas of establishing your business presence on the Internet.

Each computer that uses TCP/IP protocols is distinguished from other computers on the Internet by a unique IP address. An IP address is composed of four numbers separated by periods, and those four pieces of the IP address separated by periods are hierarchical, from left to right; for example, 198.92.135.1.

Originally, computers connected on the Internet were identified only by their IP numeric addresses. IP numeric addresses can be difficult to remember, so a text system was developed called the *domain name system (DNS).* For the most part, domain names indicate the name and type of service or organization that owns or supports the service. Domain names are organized in a hierarchical fashion, as are IP addresses, except in reverse order: the most specific (computer name) at the left and the most general top-level domain at the right. For example, the address *dave@cbs.ge.com* indicates the site is connected to a commercial domain account at ge (General Electric) and is being sent to CBS (Columbia Broadcasting System), which is owned by GE. The top-level domains on the Internet include the following:

Domain	Organization
com	Commercial and industrial organizations
edu	Education (universities and other educational organizations)
gov	Government (non-military)
mil	Military or defense organizations
org	Other organizations (non-profit and research organizations)
net	Network operation and service organizations

Some top-level domains are geographically based. For example, the geographical domain for the United States is *us*; for England, *uk*. These top-level domains can appear in a domain name address, such as *book-ware.com.us.*

Not only is it easier to work with domain names, but domain names are portable. If the computer providing a service is moved from one location to another, its network and hence its IP address will change. The domain name doesn't need to change. When the system administrator assigns the new address, he or she needs only to update the name record so that the name points to the new address.

The domain name system is an important ingredient for establishing your business presence on the Internet. It lets your business use its name as part of its address, regardless of the type of presence your business has on the Internet. Any business can register for a domain name. For most businesses, the domain name will be the business name with .com as the top-level domain specification. For example, our business is named Bookware, and it's registered under the domain name *bookware.com.* Your business can then use subdomains for routing e-mail and other services.

FYI

See Chapter 3 for information on how to register a domain name as part of getting your business wired to the Internet.

Tools of the Internet

Regardless of which side of the Internet connection you're on—client or server—several basic software tools are used for working on the Internet. These tools are based on the respective protocols that allow the client and server programs to work across the Internet. The standard applications for working on the Internet are widely available and supported by most computers connected to the Internet. Once someone is connected as a client to the Internet, he or she can work with the tools of the Internet. However, the type of connection an individual has usually determines whether the person can work with a friendly graphical user interface (GUI) version of the tool or a command-line interface.

The Internet tools let a business provide information and services online to client users. In fact, these tools define what kind of presence on the Internet a business can establish. The Internet provides a variety of tools for performing different tasks, and often users can use more than one tool to perform a given task. But the big five tools used on the Internet are as follows:

- Electronic mail, the sending and receiving of electronic messages, is the number one use of the Internet. E-mail is used not only on the Internet, but also on most commercial online services.

- Network news (USENET) is a massive, distributed conferencing system with over 5,000 ongoing conferences (called *newsgroups*) being conducted, 24 hours a day, 365 days a year. By subscribing to these newsgroups, people can communicate in forums using a messaging system similar to e-mail.

- FTP (File Transfer Protocol) is the medium that lets people send and receive files across the Internet. This popular tool is heavily used on the Internet.

- Gopher, a workhorse navigation tool, integrates a variety of Internet services into a single tool. It searches, retrieves, and displays documents from servers throughout the Internet, regardless of the type of file or server.

- World-Wide Web is the most recent and fastest growing Internet tool. It's a graphical, hypertext-based, multimedia tool that is rapidly becoming the tool of choice for users and businesses wanting to establish a presence on the Internet.

❏ INTERNET DEMOGRAPHICS

The Internet is so vast and diverse that developing a statistical profile of it and its users is like following a moving target. Several important pieces of information, however, are available that will help you evaluate the potential of the Internet. Internet demographics include types of people and organizations connected, ages and incomes of Internet users, and types of computers and operating systems connected. The following sections present a snapshot of the Internet through a mosaic of different demographic profiles.

Internet Host and Traffic Demographics

One way to get a feel for the explosive growth of the Internet is to look at the statistics associated with the operation of the Internet. These statistics include the amount of data traffic going over the NSFNET backbone, the number of host computers connected to Internet, and the distribution of the connected networks.

- The number of data packets that flowed through the NSFNET back-bone went from 85 million packets in January 1988 to 29.7 billion in May 1993.

- The number of hosts on the Internet topped 2 million in 1993, and the growth rate of hosts connected to the Internet averages about 5 percent a month. The current distribution of hosts as of January 1994 shows a growing number of commercial hosts connected to the Internet.

- The number of networks connected to the Internet has grown rapidly. Since 1990, the number of non-U.S. networks with access to the Internet has risen to nearly a third of all networks.

Internet User Demographics

Little information is currently available on typical users of the Internet. But we can glean some useful generalities from known facts about the makeup of networks connected to the Internet and their users. Internet users can be broken down into four main groups: commercial, research, government (including defense), and education. Figure 1.2 shows this breakdown. Commercial users dominate, with over 50 percent of all users, and their numbers continue to grow rapidly. Computers running MS-DOS/Windows, Macintosh, and UNIX dominate the Internet.

The one common thread among all Internet users is that they're computer users. You can extrapolate established data on computer-user demographics to help your business define Internet user profiles. Keep in mind this data can be used only as a general point of reference. Here are some important computer-user demographic figures:

- Approximately 60 percent of computer users are male and 40 percent are female. The Internet most likely has an even higher ratio of males to females because of its military-industrial complex history.

- Over 66 percent of computer users fall between the ages of 18 and 44. Another 21 percent are 45 and older.

- Over 90 percent of computer users earn $25,000 or more per year.

- Over 90 percent of computer users have some college education, a college degree, or advanced degrees.

FIGURE 1.2
The breakdown of networks connected to the Internet

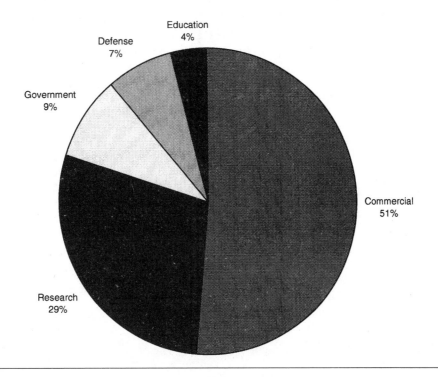

Distribution of Internet Network Registrations

Internet Services Demographics

The use of different Internet tools as measured by data traffic over the Internet backbone is shown in Figure 1.3. These figures provide only a general sense of the relative popularity of different tools. Since this is a measure of data traffic, some less data-intensive tools don't reflect the number of users.

- Of all the tools on the Internet, e-mail is used by the greatest number of people, yet e-mail ranks low in data-traffic volume. This is because e-mail is usually text-based messages that don't take up nearly as many bytes as transferring files.

- Approximately 20 percent of data traffic involves mail and network news traffic. Like e-mail, network news is a text-based messaging system, so its data-traffic volume is low, but the number of users is high.

- The biggest volume of network traffic is generated by people using FTP, with approximately 45 to 50 percent of current network traffic involving file exchange. This figure reflects the fact that transferring files is a data-intensive process.

- Interactive traffic, which is centered around using Telnet (a remote login program), accounts for about 6 percent of Internet data traffic.

- Looking up users using domain name lookup accounts for around 3 percent of traffic.

- Gopher and World-Wide Web together account for about 25 percent of network traffic. This is the fastest growing category of data traffic.

FIGURE 1.3
Percent of Internet traffic by categories of Internet services

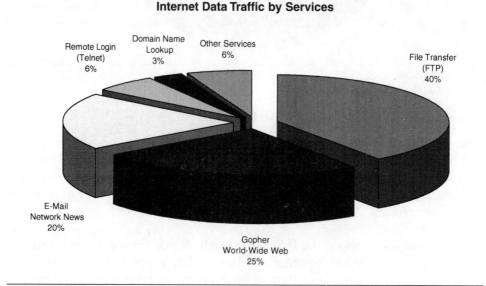

Internet Data Traffic by Services

Remote Login (Telnet) 6%

Domain Name Lookup 3%

Other Services 6%

File Transfer (FTP) 40%

E-Mail Network News 20%

Gopher World-Wide Web 25%

❏ THE MARCH TOWARD COMMERCIALIZATION OF THE INTERNET

As explained earlier, the Internet was born from the R&D demands of the military-industrial complex, acting as the communications conduit for the government, universities, and large defense-industry companies. The role of the federal government in the development and financing of the Internet kept the Internet noncommercial until the last few years. Today, not only are most governmental barriers coming down, but some important commercialization initiatives and projects are under way. The following sections take a look at the major players participating in the march toward commercialization of the Internet. Because commercialization of the Internet is rapidly moving forward, new players will emerge.

NSF and NREN

The National Science Foundation (NSF), a U.S. government organization, operates a significant chunk of the Internet's backbone. This backbone is called NSFNET. Because the purpose of NSF is research, it originally set restrictions on the use of its backbone, such as the transferring of commercial data. Until recently, the most quoted policy for acceptable use on the Internet was NSFNET's acceptable use policy (AUP), which basically stated that transmission of commercial information or traffic was not allowed across the NSFNET backbone, whereas all information in support of academic and research activities was acceptable. But because the Internet is a packet-switching network that automatically routes packets across different networks, these restrictions were virtually unenforceable. In 1990, the policy changed to cover only traffic that flowed from NSF-funded organizations.

The National Research and Education Network (NREN) is expected to build on and eventually replace the NSF's involvement in the Internet. NREN was authorized by the High Performance Computing Act of 1991, which was promoted by then-Senator Al Gore of Tennessee. This act will pump $2.9 billion of government funds into building a high-speed Internet backbone network. NREN also promises to abolish any remaining vestiges of anticommercial user policies and open the Internet to a broad spectrum of commercial, government, and educational users.

CIX, CO+RE, and CoREN

Leading commercial Internet service providers have joined forces to create a commercial alternative to the NSFNET backbone. These service providers formed CIX (commercial Internet exchange), which is pronounced "kicks." CIX was established in 1991 to provide a nonrestrictive path for business traffic to cross the Internet without the use of the NSFNET infrastructure. Also in 1991, Advanced Network and Service Inc. (ANS), the company that was formed to provide the National Science Foundation's high-speed backbone, announced a commercial service called CO+RE (commercial plus research and educational). Several regional network service providers have expanded their scope of service to businesses by joining with MCI Communications Corporation in a group called CoREN (Corporation for Regional and Enterprise Networking). These new associations have been a formidable force in changing the Internet's focus from an academic to a business communications medium.

CommerceNet and EINnet

One of the most exciting and promising commercialization projects is CommerceNet. Launched in April 1994, CommerceNet was the first large-scale market trial for virtual commerce on the Internet. CommerceNet was created by a nonprofit consortium funded by a grant from the U.S. government's Technology Reinvestment Project, the state of California, and member companies. CommerceNet's goals are to provide solutions to several problems that have deterred businesses from doing business on the Internet, primarily the lack of a standard secure means of transmitting proprietary data or financial information and a centralized authority to oversee transactions. The principal vehicle for working on CommerceNet is an enhanced version of the leading World-Wide Web client called Mosaic. World-Wide Web is a graphical hypertext environment that supports multimedia presentations, including audio, video, text, and graphics. Figure 1.4 shows the CommerceNet virtual mall as it appears to Internet users. The key enhancement to World-Wide Web by CommerceNet is that it includes public-key cryptography that allows authentication as well as data encryption to protect business transactions of all kinds. Digital signatures ensure that important information is delivered uncorrupted and untampered with. The goal is to enable buyers and sellers to meet on the network and safely exchange sensitive information—such as credit-card numbers, bid amounts, and legally enforceable contracts—and have financial institutions transfer the funds.

FIGURE 1.4

The CommerceNet Internet presence

Another commercialization project is being put together by Sprint, Microelectronics and Computer Technology Corporation (MCC). The goal is to offer a platform for virtual commerce services on the Internet. MCC has been working for several years to define and develop the tools for a fully functional commercial application on the Internet—one that includes directory services, security, advanced e-mail, and remittance capabilities based on open standards. EINet plans to add features necessary to make the Internet the preferred means for all companies to communicate, develop partnerships, carry out research projects, and conduct their buying and selling with each other.

The National Information Infrastructure

Shortly after taking office, President Clinton announced a plan to stimulate development of an advanced electronic infrastructure that promised government funding for high-speed networking. The development of this high-speed network has been dubbed the national information infrastructure. This infrastructure can be compared to the building of the national highway infrastructure in the 1950s. The U.S. government funded the national highway system because no commercial incentive existed to build the highways. But after the highways were in place, they had a tremendous effect on the economy, interstate commerce, and the social structure of the country. Similarly, the development of a national data highway will lead to commercial development in many areas. Roadside services are the big growth area of the Internet. New components will be added to the Internet as telephone, cable, and entertainment companies try to stake their claims.

The Falling Cost of Establishing an Internet Presence

The relaxation of policies to allow commerce on the Internet has spurred a new generation of Internet access providers that are targeting their services to businesses. Competition among service providers is making more sophisticated connection options affordable to many businesses that were previously excluded. Another emerging industry allowing businesses affordable access to the millions of Internet users is the server service industry. *Server services*, also referred to as service bureaus, are companies that sell server space and services. Server services give businesses an affordable avenue to publish on the Internet or establish virtual storefronts by selling space on servers they operate. The expensive overhead of hardware and software systems, high-speed data lines, and expertise involved in setting up and maintaining a server on the Internet is spread over many businesses.

❏ CONDUCTING VIRTUAL COMMERCE ON THE INTERNET

Internet business opportunities can be broken down into two broad categories: marketing and internal operations. On the marketing front, the Internet provides a collection of tools for a new kind of interactive advertising, customer service and support, and product information. For internal operations, the Internet provides a variety of tools for moving information, collaboration and development, and vendor support to make your business operate more efficiently and profitably. Using the Internet and its key tools, your business can do the following:

- Communicate with customers instantly, including sending requested information on demand to customers using electronic mail

- Collaborate with colleagues by exchanging electronic mail and files

- Promote your business by posting information to widely distributed Internet forums

- Publish information such as brochures, newsletters, and catalogs online

- Create virtual storefronts to generate sales directly from the Internet

- Distribute files in any format quickly and conveniently to anyone or a select group

- Access the vast resources available on the Internet, such as people, information and program files, online databases, libraries, and so on.

The Internet Business Climate

The Internet is no longer the exclusively academic and technical network it once was. However, it's not completely open for conducting business. The Internet still has customs, conventions, and taboos carried over from its early noncommercial days. For example, one of the most notorious areas where commercial activities are frowned upon is network news. Still, even this bastion of the Internet's technical past is changing to reflect the commercialization wave on the Internet.

The key rule that defines the business climate of the Internet is that in-your-face activities, such as unsolicited communications, are not well accepted. On-demand activities such as setting up a virtual storefront for

Internet users are accepted. If you operate your business within the on-demand context and also take a content-based marketing approach, it will be accepted by Internet users as a resource.

Sensitivity to the Internet's culture will spell success for doing virtual business in cyberspace. It's helpful to think of conducting business on the Internet as doing business in a foreign country. As with any foreign market, your business must be aware of customs and conventions. The key to effective Internet marketing is taking the time to learn what is and what is not acceptable on the Internet. Different tools have different conventions of acceptable use.

Other factors play a role in defining the current climate for conducting business on the Internet. Most notable are the issues of privacy and security in electronic communications. Many Internet users are reluctant to send credit-card information via electronic mail. This is because the Internet is a packet-based network, which means an electronic mail message gets routed through many different nodes before reaching its destination. The risk of having your credit-card number intercepted on the Internet is perceived as being potentially higher than on the phone. But as people become more familiar with the medium, and as Internet businesses continue to provide different methods of securing credit-card transactions, the benefits will outweigh the risks.

Interactive Internet Marketing

As a marketing medium, the Internet is different from traditional mass media. Ginsu knife-style advertising does not go over well on the Internet. Soliciting sales using traditional TV, radio, or paper-based advertising or invasive telemarketing techniques will cause your business to be flooded with *flames* (irate electronic mail or publicly posted messages), and you will be discredited throughout the Internet within a few hours or days. Unsolicited or intrusive advertising, such as a mass electronic mailing, is a dangerous area of marketing on the Internet that can work against you, rather than for you.

Content-based marketing, which is the packaging of your business information as a resource, is the rule of the Internet. The Internet community appreciates quality, filtered information. Find a way to add value to your message. For example, a promotional message can be expressed within a commentary on industry trends. Businesses need to take a new proactive approach when communicating to the Internet community. To be fully accepted by the majority of Internet users, a business needs to become interactive and participate in the virtual communities it wishes to reach. Unlike other advertising media, the Internet is fully bidirectional. Pontificating from the lofty heights of corporate sales and marketing offices only alienates the typical Internet user.

To evaluate the economics of Internet-based marketing, you should compare the costs of traditional marketing options. For example, you need to compare the cost of placing an advertisement in a magazine with the cost of presenting information online. In many cases, using the services of the Internet as an advertising medium is considerably cheaper and offers more interaction with the customer. However, the biggest cost of Internet marketing is not the cost of presenting the information, but the labor required to dialog with the market. This is because the Internet is not one vast, homogeneous market, but a constellation of different virtual communities. Interactively participating in these virtual communities one by one will help establish your Internet business presence and let you successfully tap into the Internet market as a whole.

Chapter 2

Developing Your Internet Business Plan

Establishing a virtual business presence on the Internet involves a journey through a maze of topics. Before you start on your journey, you need to develop an effective Internet business plan. This plan puts all the important elements involved in getting your business on the Internet into a meaningful whole. From this starting point, you can then proceed in an orderly fashion through the specifics. This chapter identifies and explains the key components for establishing an affordable and effective Internet business presence. It covers the mental framework you need to guide you through the process, an overview of getting your business wired to the Internet, an explanation of using a server presence to provide services to Internet users, and an overview of the key Internet tools for conducting commerce on Internet.

❑ THE ZEN OF ESTABLISHING AN INTERNET BUSINESS PRESENCE

To establish a business presence on the Internet, you need to erect a virtual presence for your business in cyberspace. The best approach to establishing a presence for your business on the Internet is to view it as a modular and evolutionary process. It requires navigating through a myriad of technical, financial, and other issues.

Virtual commerce on the Internet is a new business frontier because all the technology, players, prices, and services involved in establishing a business presence are in a constant state of flux. The good news is that the general trend in prices is downward, and the improvement in services is upward.

As critical mass is achieved, competition increases, and technology improves, establishing a business presence on the Internet will get better and easier.

To develop and implement an Internet business plan, you must also integrate working on the Internet into your existing ways of doing business. Because doing business in cyberspace is a new concept, expect a period of trial and error. As your business integrates the Internet into its operations, you can make changes from a more informed perspective. The best way to manage your Internet implementation is to consistently evaluate, integrate, monitor, and modify. The following are some general guidelines to keep in mind as you develop your plan:

- Think of your Internet presence as an investment in future positioning of your business.

- Be patient, and stay committed to your plan.

- Build your presence one step at a time, with a realistic projection of future needs and trends.

- View your presence on the Internet as a convenience to a growing Internet customer base.

- Be prepared to run a lot of financial calculations when determining your options. Most services you need to establish a presence on the Internet are priced individually—don't expect to find package deals.

Being a User and Provider of Internet Services

A business on the Internet will most likely be acting as a user of Internet services as well as a provider of services to other Internet users. As we mentioned in Chapter 1, the computer site that provides resources, such as information, programs, and services to its customers is known as a server (also referred to as a host computer). The computers that connect to the server to access its resources are clients. Figure 2.1 shows the relationship between client and server activities. This client/server structure of networking is the basis of the Internet and defines the difference between a user and an information provider. A full-fledged Internet business presence will involve both elements. For example, a business might use FTP (the file-transfer tool) to obtain files but also provide a server site for users to get files.

FIGURE 2.1
The client and server sides of an Internet business presence

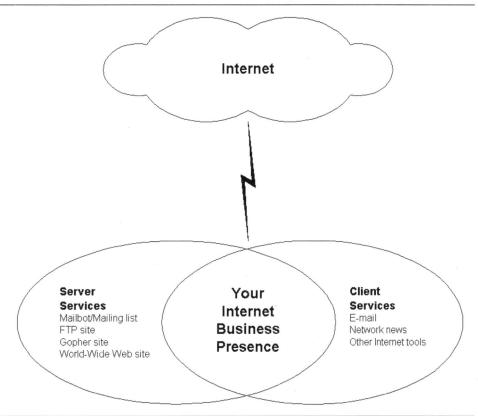

Put Yourself in the Driver's Seat

When it comes to establishing a presence on the Internet, knowledge is power. As a business decision maker, you need to understand the issues, even if you plan to have others do the work for you. If you don't understand the tools and options of the Internet, then technical people (consultants, server services, service providers) will decide your business objectives, which can be costly. Keep the technical people where they belong—advising and applying your Internet business strategy, not deciding it. This book gives you the information you need to stay in the driver's seat throughout the process of establishing your business's Internet presence.

Use Your Business Judgment

One of the most exciting opportunities the Internet delivers is that it levels the playing field for businesses. Just about any business can establish an impressive presence that rivals that of a Fortune 500 corporation, but at a fraction of the cost. But it's easy to let the popularized, mass-media version of the growth and opportunity of the Internet cloud your better business judgment. The Internet is a communications and data-movement medium. How you use it determines its effectiveness to your business. Establishing an Internet presence demands you use the time-honored principles that drive any business:

- Reduce the costs of doing business
- Increase the ability to market effectively
- Gain an advantage over the competition

❑ GETTING YOUR BUSINESS WIRED TO THE INTERNET

A *service provider* is a company or other organization that offers connections to the Internet through its computers, which are part of the Internet. The type of connection you have to the Internet determines which options are available to your business. The lowest level of client access to the Internet are the shell and menu accounts. A *shell account* or a *menu account* lets a user dial up the service provider's computers using a modem and standard communications software. When the user connects using a shell or menu account, its computers are not directly connected to the Internet. The service provider's computer acts as the client that users control from their remote location. In most cases, these accounts require working with the service provider's operating system, which is usually UNIX. As an alternative to working with UNIX, many service providers offer menu-based accounts, and a few now offer graphical-based accounts. These types of accounts are too limited for establishing a full-fledged business presence on the Internet.

All computers that are directly connected to the Internet have one thing in common. They use the TCP/IP protocol to communicate with one another. The starting point for establishing a business presence is the IP (Internet Protocol) account. The IP class of accounts offer a true Internet connection that includes your own Internet domain name address. At the low end of the IP hierarchy, you can start out with a low-cost, single-user dial-up account. On the high end of the IP hierarchy is the dedicated connection, which consists of a leased, high-speed data transmission line with multiple networked (LAN) users connected to a multitasking workstation or router. Using an IP connection to establish your business presence on the Internet has the following advantages:

- Your business has access to the Internet using programs based on the native operating environment of your computers. For example, if you're using Windows, you use a Windows program to work with Internet tools, saving the cost of training people to work with UNIX. Figure 2.2 shows what the Internet looks like using an IP account with Windows.

- You can identify your company with a unique domain name that you choose. A domain name lets you capitalize on any name recognition associated with your business name. For example, our business name is Bookware, and our domain name is bookware.com. Your domain name is completely portable, meaning you can change your IP account configuration without changing your domain name.

- You can add electronic mail addresses under your domain name. For example, using a LAN IP account with the domain name bookware.com, you can add electronic mail addresses for different functions, such as orders@bookware.com, or electronic mail addresses for individuals, such as dangell@bookware.com, or bheslop@bookware.com.

- You can add server services under your business domain name.

FYI

See Chapter 3 for information on getting your business wired with an IP account.

FIGURE 2.2

An IP account view of the Internet

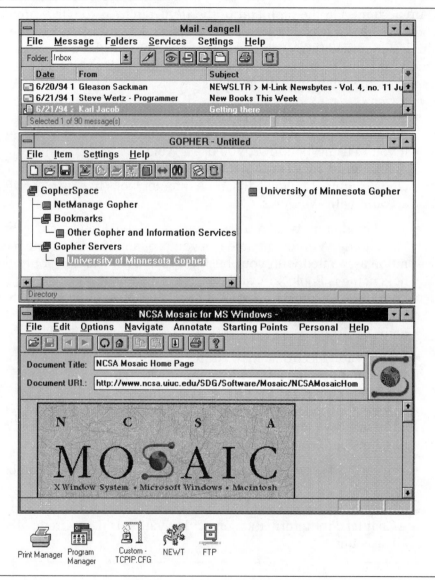

❏ ESTABLISHING A SERVER PRESENCE ON THE INTERNET

To establish a server presence on the Internet, you can take two paths: do it yourself, or rent space on a server service's server. The do-it-yourself server approach requires a UNIX server, a dedicated connection, a leased, high-volume data transmission line for handling incoming traffic, and technical expertise to put it all together. It offers the most flexibility in the long run, but is currently a prohibitively expensive proposition for many businesses.

Because of the complexity and expense of setting up and maintaining a server on your own, you can instead use a server service to set up and maintain a server presence on the Internet for your business. The server service acts as a kind of time-sharing service to spread the cost of establishing a server over many businesses. These servers support the tools used by Internet users. For example, a server service can create a World-Wide Web server presence that would let Internet users view online graphic-based information about your business. You can publish information or operate a virtual storefront. Your server presence can be part of the server services' virtual mall or operate as a stand-alone site on the Internet.

FYI

See Chapter 4 for information on establishing a server presence on the Internet.

❏ THE BIG FIVE INTERNET TOOLS THAT DEFINE YOUR BUSINESS PRESENCE

What your business can accomplish on the Internet is defined largely by the tools supported by the Internet. These tools are the applications and protocols that define the types of activities that can be performed on the Internet from both a client and a server perspective. Selecting and working with the right tools is at the heart of a successful Internet business strategy. Although many tools are available on the Internet, five essential tools will define your business presence on the Internet: e-mail, network news, FTP, Gopher, and World-Wide Web. The following sections give a brief overview of these tools and explain other tools that you should know about.

The Mother of All Tools: Electronic Mail

E-mail is the number one use of the Internet. Every user account on the Internet comes with e-mail capabilities. Beyond the 38 million people connected to the Internet, the Internet mail system also includes gateways that extend beyond the Internet to include virtually every commercial network, including CompuServe, America Online, Delphi, MCI Mail, and others.

E-mail is rapidly becoming the dominant form of business communications and customer interaction. Businesses connecting their customer services and employees to the Internet electronic mail system open up new marketing, collaboration, and efficiency opportunities. Establishing an e-mail presence is linked with getting your business wired, because your e-mail accounts are set up as part of establishing your connection. You'll need to get a solid grasp of your e-mail options before you shop for your Internet connection. Different service providers offer different e-mail options. If you run a small business, pay attention to getting multiple e-mail addresses under one domain name.

Besides using e-mail for one-on-one internal and customer communications, your business can establish an e-mail server presence. E-mail servers let your business send out information automatically, such as a newsletter or press release, to anyone requesting it or subscribing to your service.

FYI

See Chapter 3 for information on establishing an e-mail presence for your business. Chapter 5 explains how to manage your business e-mail and establish an e-mail server presence on the Internet.

Promoting Your Business via Network News

Network news (also known as USENET) is a distributed conferencing system transported over the Internet. The more than 5,000 discussion groups offer a newsgroup for almost every taste. People who subscribe to newsgroups communicate using a publicly broadcast messaging system that is similar in structure to e-mail. The news articles can be serious or frivolous. Network news offers a medium for promoting your server services on the Internet. However, to use this medium you must be aware of the network news culture and its attitude toward unsolicited advertising. But even this tool is opening up to allow business posting of product announcements and other forms of information-based advertising in certain areas. Businesses can contribute to newsgroups and in some cases create their own news-groups.

FYI ————————————————————————————

See Chapter 6 for more information on using network news to find answers to your questions or help notify others of your presence on the Internet.

Moving Information with FTP

The File Transfer Protocol (FTP) is the medium that lets people send and receive files across the Internet using the FTP program. Almost everyone connected to the Internet has access to FTP. For businesses, FTP offers affordable opportunities for setting up an FTP server to share information with all Internet users or with a select group of people. Your business can use FTP as an internal business tool, sending and receiving sales orders, manuscripts, reports, and so on across the Internet. Creating a public FTP server (called an *anonymous FTP site*) is an excellent and easy way to share files, such as catalogs, price lists, technical support documents, and other information with customers. Thousands of public anonymous FTP sites already exist on the Internet; they are used to distribute all kinds of files, such as graphics, programs, and information. If it can be stored in a file, it can be distributed via FTP. Creating your own public or private FTP site is a cost-effective way to make large quantities of information available inter-nally or to all Internet users.

FYI ————————————————————————————

See Chapter 7 for more information on FTP and establishing an FTP server presence on the Internet.

Gopher: The Internet Workhorse

Gopher is one of the leading workhorses of the Internet. It's an information system used to organize and distribute information on thousands of servers across the Internet. Gopher integrates a variety of Internet services—such as FTP, Telnet, and WAIS—into a single tool. It lets users search the Internet for

FIGURE 2.3
A typical Gopher site

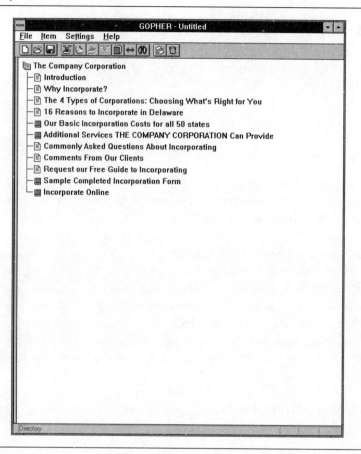

information using keywords. Gopher not only does searches, it retrieves and displays documents from servers throughout the Internet. Establishing a server presence in Gopherspace links your business to a network of Gopher servers where millions of Internet users can quickly find your site. Once they arrive at your site, they can read published information or conduct business at a virtual storefront. Figure 2.3 shows a typical Gopher site.

FYI

See Chapter 8 for more information on establishing a Gopher server presence.

FIGURE 2.4
A typical World-Wide Web site

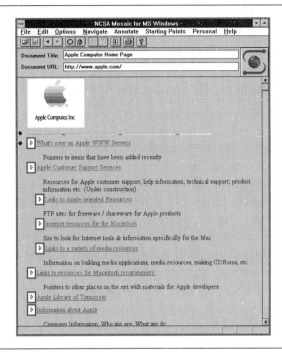

A Slick Internet Presence with World-Wide Web

The most recent and fastest growing addition to the family of Internet tools is the World-Wide Web, commonly known as the Web. The Web, with its friendly, graphical interface, is changing the face of the Internet from a barren command-line interface to a slick hypermedia (hypertext and multimedia) environment. For example, a client using a multimedia-capable computer can view graphic and video files and listen to an audio file, as well as retrieve information from just about any Internet source. Millions of Internet users and organizations are converting to this new infrastructure for online publishing and conducting virtual commerce. To access and use the full capabilities of a World-Wide Web server, the Internet user must have an IP connection. Figure 2.4 shows a sample World-Wide Web site as viewed using the Mosaic program.

FYI ──
See Chapter 9 for more information on working with World-Wide Web.

❑ OTHER TOOLS WORTH MENTIONING

Beyond the big five Internet tools, there are a few other useful tools that any business establishing a presence on the Internet will want to know about. These include telnet, WAIS, finger, chat and conferencing tools.

Computing by Remote Control with Telnet

The Telnet protocol allows Internet users to remotely log onto other computers to use their services. For example, Internet users can use telnet to log onto a server that is running a database. Once they're connected, they can operate the database as if they were sitting at a terminal at the local site. Telnet sites are more sophisticated than anonymous FTP sites because they allow users to work on that computer to perform searches, retrieval, and other real-time tasks. The telnet program is often used in conjunction with other tools on the Internet. For example, people can use telnet to get to a Gopher server that acts as the gateway to all kinds of services on the Internet. Although the telnet program is used by Internet users, establishing a server presence based on this tool is not widely offered.

Information Retrieval via English Queries

WAIS (pronounced "ways") stands for wide-area information server. The WAIS program is an information-retrieval system that allows information from different databases, called *sources,* to be easily searched using simple English queries. WAIS can search any type of material, such as catalogs, lists of products, services, and prices; databases, such as employee addresses; and documents, such as press releases, product reviews, and brochures. Although WAIS is a powerful tool, in most cases it is invisible to the user. For example, you can access a WAIS server using Gopher and World-Wide Web clients. Some WAIS clients are available, but most Internet users access WAIS using other tools. WAIS lets Internet users search and retrieve information from sources regardless of where that information resides on the Internet. It provides a solution to making a large pool of information in database form available online. At this writing, most server services do not offer WAIS database support as a packaged solution as they do for Gopher and the Web. This is likely to change as WAIS servers become more mainstream and more traditional publishers begin using WAIS to distribute their work. For example, Dow Jones has announced it will be distributing the *Wall Street Journal* and same-day *New York Times* on the Internet through a WAIS server.

Fingering People and Companies on the Internet

The finger command is a widely used Internet facility that allows people to view information from a user's login file. It lets Internet users find out someone's login name (hence the e-mail address) plus his or her full name, the last time the person was logged on, and other information. As a business, you can offer people a way to find out about your business when they finger your domain name.

For example, our company, Bookware, uses the bookware.com domain name. A user enters the command finger *bookware.com* to display a part of the login file, which might look like:

Login name: bookware.com   In real life: Bookware

Home:/u41/bookware   Shell:/bin/ksh

Last login Mon Oct 31 12:43:02 on tyyb

No unread mail.

No plan.

Finger information can also display two optional fields of information called Project and Plan. These fields are linked to two hidden text files .project and .plan that you can easily create. These files can be a handy source of information for people that are trying to contact your business. The contents of these hidden text files are displayed if someone on the Internet fingers your domain name. The finger command displays only one line for the Project. The Plan file can include as many lines of text as you want, although you should try to keep it to a single screenful. If the file is longer than a screenful, it will scroll by faster than it can be read. The following shows an example of what can be displayed using a .project and .plan file when an Internet user fingers *bookware.com*.

Login name: bookware.com   In real life: Bookware

Home:/u41/bookware   Shell:/bin/ksh

Last login Mon Oct 31 12:43:02 on tyyb

No unread mail.

Project: Technical Communication Services

Plan:

We (David Angell and Brent Heslop) are partners in Bookware, which is located in Silicon Valley. We have written 12 books for major publishers on a range of PC and workstation topics, and we are frequent contributors to popular computer industry periodicals. You can contact us at:

Bookware
1739 Begen Ave.
Mountain View, CA 94040
Voice: (415) 967-0559
Fax: (415) 967-8283
E-Mail: dangell@bookware.com or bheslop@bookware.com

Private Online Conferencing

Operating in a manner similar to network news, conferencing tools let you participate in ongoing discussions via messages posted and linked together to create dialog. It's not the same as chatting, where people carry on a discussion in real-time with dialog typed directly among the participants. But conferencing allows groups of geographically dispersed people to carry on ongoing, private discussions and have a text record to work with. These discussions continue on even if the participants aren't logged on at the same time. The Meta Network operates an affordable online private conferencing service that businesses can use to set up conferences. Participants use the telnet program to remotely login to the Meta host system, and then enter a conference by using a private user ID. A moderator manages the conference, performing the role of a leader in face-to-face meetings. Discussions can include a few people or hundreds. A participant reads an item (message), and if he or she responds, the response is appended to the message. All these items are linked and displayed as an ongoing discussion.

Throughout the Internet there are hundreds of real-time chatting facilities, most of which are based on the IRC (Internet Relay Chat). Up until recently IRC facilities have been used for non-business-related discussions. However, there is growing interest in using Internet chat facilities for private, real-time business collaboration and conferencing. Expect to see some implementation of real-time chatting within a friendly GUI environment like that of the World-Wide Web.

Chapter 3

❏ ❏ ❏

Getting Your Business Wired to the Internet

Getting your business wired to the Internet is a process that is fraught with technical, financial, and strategic complexities. It involves a series of inter-connected decisions based on sorting through a myriad of available options, such as setting up the right type of Internet account, selecting and setting up the TCP/IP software, and choosing the right type of telecommunications line. Unfortunately, these options aren't packaged as off-the-shelf solutions, prices are constantly changing, and new technologies are emerging. To make things even more challenging, you'll also need to anticipate your future business activities on the Internet to make the right decisions today. Feeling overwhelmed? Relax. This chapter walks you through the necessary steps and points out pitfalls along the way to help you make the right Internet connection for your business.

❏ ESTABLISHING YOUR BUSINESS DOMAIN NAME

As explained in Chapter 1, the Internet uses an addressing scheme called the *domain name system (DNS)*. For the most part, domain names indicate the name and type of service or organization that owns or supports the service. When you establish a connection, you choose a domain name that is your unique Internet address. In most cases, your domain name is the same as your business name. A domain name lets you capitalize on any name recognition associated with your business name. Your business e-mail addresses are tied to your domain name. For example, our business name is Bookware, our domain name is *bookware.com*, and our e-mail addresses end with *book-ware.com*. Because domain names are registered, you need to make sure the name you want is available. When you establish an account, a domain name is registered by your service provider or server service with an organization called InterNIC.

Defining Your Domain Name

Domain names are organized in a hierarchical fashion with the most specific (computer name) at the left and the most general top-level domain to the right. For example, *dangell@bookware.com* translates to the user *dangell* at the *bookware* host computer, and *.com* is the top-level domain specification. A domain name consists of two or more alphanumeric fields, separated by a period (called a dot). No spaces are allowed in a domain name, but you can use the underscore (_) to indicate a space. Each field consists of some combination of the letters A through Z (in either uppercase or lowercase), the digits 0 through 9, and the hyphen (-). Be sure not to include the period (.), at sign (@), percent sign (%), or exclamation point (!). These characters are used by domain name servers and other network systems to construct e-mail addresses. Domain names are case-insensitive, so it doesn't matter whether letters are uppercase or lowercase.

In most cases, businesses register using the *.com* top-level domain, which stands for commercial. However, businesses can also register under the *.us* top-level domain, which is a geographical domain for the United States. In most cases, you don't want to limit yourself to a geographical domain name. However, if you can't use your business name as a *.com* domain name because it has already been used, you may want to use the *.us* top-level domain. For example, if *bookware.com* had already been taken, we could have tried *bookware.us*. If you are running a nonprofit organization, you may be able to use the *.org* top-level domain.

As explained in Chapter 1, two main types of addresses work together on the Internet: *domain names* and *IP addresses*. Each computer that uses TCP/IP protocols is distinguished from other computers on the Internet by a unique IP address. An IP address is four numbers separated by periods; for example, 198.92.135.1. If you plan to connect a LAN to the Internet, you need a class C IP address, which lets you subdivide your domain name. You can use a class C IP address to supply a name for each of your computers, or you can create subdomains for routing e-mail and other services. Many large organizations have multiple levels of subdomains. Figure 3.1 shows the breakdown of a typical Internet address with multiple subdomains. The field on the right is the name of the top-level domain, which is the owner name of the domain. The other fields can specify one or more levels of subdomain, such as a computer name, department, user name, and so on. Only the domain name needs to be registered. For example, if you're registering *bookware.com*, you do not need to register *sales.bookware.com*.

FIGURE 3.1
The parts of a typical domain name with multiple subdomains

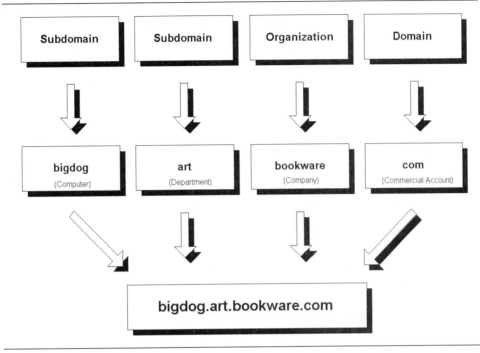

Some service providers, such as PSI, use dynamic IP account addresses in dial-up accounts to allow for multiple e-mail addresses for single-user IP accounts and for security purposes. When you connect to the service provider with a dynamic IP address, the IP address can change, but your domain name always stays the same.

Checking the Availability of a Domain Name

Registration of domain names is handled by InterNIC, a collaborative project of three organizations that is supported by the National Science Foundation. Registration services are handled by Network Solutions, based in Virginia. Names are registered on a first-come, first-served basis. Registering a domain name implies no legal ownership of the name. For example, you may be able to register a domain name that is the name of another company, but that company can send its lawyers after you for using its trade name. A good example of this is the legal suit Viacom Inc.'s MTV music television channel brought against Adam Curry for using *mtv.com* as his domain name. Here are three ways you can check to see if a domain name is taken:

- The easiest way to find out if a specific name is unavailable is to call registration services directly at (703) 742-4777 or fax (703) 742-4811. When the registration representative answers, ask to check the status of a domain name. In some cases, a name may be registered but not yet put through the system.

- If you have an e-mail account that has access to the Internet, such as America Online, CompuServe, or MCI Mail, you can check the domain name by sending an e-mail message to *postmaster@rs.internic.net*.

- If you have access to an Internet account, you can use Telnet to access the InterNIC's online database to search domain names yourself. To do this, use Telnet to access *rs.internic.net*. At the system prompt on the InterNIC computer, type *whois*. At the prompt, you can type the domain names you want to check. The database searches for the domain name. If no match is found, it's available. If a match is found, information is displayed about the company that has registered the domain name, as shown in Figure 3.2. You can repeat this process as often as you want. When you are done, type *logout*.

FIGURE 3.2

Sample information display of a registered domain name

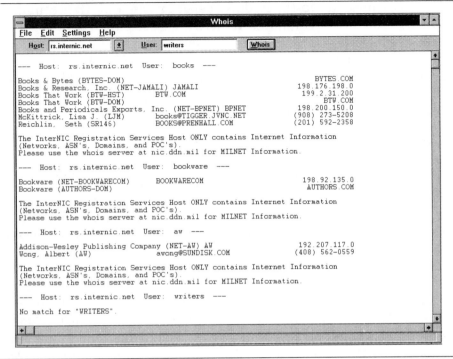

Registering a Domain Name

Once you determine your domain name and you decide on your service provider, the service provider will apply for the domain name with InterNIC registration services. Domain name registration is usually done by the service provider because it needs to supply the IP addresses that are used to route information to your domain name. These IP addresses include one for the service provider's host computer system, and another IP address is assigned to the host at your end of the connection. Registering a domain name without these IP addresses is discouraged by the InterNIC but can be done. This is because at the time the InterNIC registers your domain name, the mapping to the IP addresses is also entered in the database. If no IP addresses are added, the entry is incomplete.

❑ SPEAKING TCP/IP

To make a connection to the Internet using any type of IP account, you must first make your computer or network speak the language of the Internet, which is TCP/IP (Transmission Control Protocol/Internet Protocol). To work with an IP account, you need a TCP/IP software program, called a *TCP/IP stack,* so your computer can speak and understand the language of the Internet. TCP/IP is already built into most versions of UNIX. Microsoft has announced that an upcoming version of Windows will include a 32-bit TCP/IP stack and will have dial-up PPP built in. (PPP is explained in the following section.) A TCP/IP stack will most likely be built into future versions of the Macintosh operating system as well.

For now, if your business is using PCs and Macintoshes, commercial and public-domain software programs include a TCP/IP stack. If you are running Windows, a special program known as *WinSock* specifies a set of calls that applications can make to interface with your TCP/IP stack. This lets any program that uses the WinSock interface access your TCP/IP stack. Most TCP/IP programs for Windows include the TCP/IP stack and WinSock. Besides providing the familiar interface of your local computer system for working on the Internet, most TCP/IP packages include graphical-based Internet tools, such as e-mail, FTP, and Gopher. Using a graphical-front-end is a lot easier than working with UNIX commands. For PCs running Windows, NetManage offers a popular TCP/IP product named Chameleon. If you're using a Macintosh, MacTCP is the de facto standard. TCP/IP tools are also being added to popular communications programs. For example, MicroPhone for the Macintosh includes MacTCP, MacSLIP, Telnet, FTP (Fetch), and an Internet News program.

Each computer that is going to access the Internet must have a TCP/IP program running on it. Setting up TCP/IP software involves complexities that can frustrate even the technically savvy user. There is a strong case to be made for commercial packages that offer documentation and technical support.

Some service providers, such as Netcom, are providing TCP/IP programs in conjunction with establishing an IP account. Netcom's NetCruiser streamlines the process of getting started with a single-user IP account and provides a graphical front-end for working on the Internet. Another TCP/IP program, called Pipeline, is being bundled with accounts by service providers. See the appendix for more information on TCP/IP programs.

The Big Three IP Account Types

You can choose from three types of IP accounts: PPP, which stands for Point to Point Protocol; SLIP, which stands for Serial Link Internet Protocol; and CSLIP, which stands for Compressed SLIP. Not all service providers support all these IP account types. PPP is the connection of choice because it is the standard Internet serial-line protocol for modem-to-modem communications. PPP includes error-detection facilities to establish an error-free transfer of data, so it is more reliable than SLIP. (If these terms are unfamiliar, refer to the glossary.) Besides these features, PPP supports more protocols and is faster than SLIP. PPP can be used with other protocols, such as Novell IPX or AppleTalk. Because PPP is more complex than SLIP and SLIP is included in most UNIX systems, PPP has not been as widely implemented as SLIP. If your service provider doesn't offer PPP, see if you can use CSLIP. CSLIP compresses the IP address information in data files for faster file transfers. If you plan to transfer large files frequently, CSLIP can save you time. Some service providers will want to know if you want compression on or off for your IP account, so you will need to know whether your PPP/SLIP package supports compression.

Most Windows TCP/IP programs include support for PPP/SLIP. The standard Macintosh TCP/IP program, MacTCP, comes by itself and doesn't include PPP/SLIP support. Fortunately, MacTCP is bundled with most commercial Macintosh PPP/SLIP programs. For example, VersaTerm from Synergy Software and TCP/Connect II from InterCon both include MacTCP. Two popular Macintosh SLIP programs are InterSLIP from InterCon and MacSLIP from Trisoft. On the UNIX platform, which doesn't include built-in PPP support, MorningStar PPP/SLIP has the market sewn up. Before you purchase a TCP/IP and PPP/SLIP software package, check to see if it offers all the features you want. For more information on TCP/IP programs, see the appendix.

❑ SETTING UP A SINGLE-USER IP CONNECTION

The single-user IP account is the least expensive type of IP account. This type of IP account offers several configuration options. Which options you choose depend on the amount of time you'll be using your Internet connection. The single-user, dial-up IP account allows only one person to use it at any given time, but it can be used on one computer and shared by different people in a small business. You can even add additional electronic mailboxes to this account so that several people can have e-mail addresses connected to the business domain name. For example, two people can have separate e-mail addresses, such as *dangell@bookware.com* and *bheslop@bookware.com*. A single-user, dial-up IP account is usually used with a high-speed modem over standard voice-grade telephone lines, referred to as POTS (plain old telephone service). However, ISDN service is becoming available in many areas, which promises low-cost, high-speed digital telecommunications. Working with different telecommunications-line options is explained later in this chapter.

Shopping for a Single IP Account

Different service providers offer different pricing and service options for single IP accounts, and each uses different terminology. For example, Netcom calls a single IP account a PNC (personal network connection), but PSI calls it a host-dial account. When you shop around for your IP account, consider the cost of the account and the cost of connecting to it. Most service providers will charge a setup fee to establish the account, which can include a variety of services, such as providing a TCP/IP software package and registering the domain name.

You need to estimate your usage of an IP account before you can project your costs. Generally, when estimating your projected use, be liberal. Over the first few months, as you or the users sharing the IP account get used to working with it, the volume of activity will increase. To make the best cost comparison between service providers and different telecommunications charges, estimate the time your business will be connected to the Internet. Determine the tasks you'll be performing, which most likely will be working with e-mail, sending and retrieving files, and accessing resources on the Internet. A low-volume Internet user might be connected from 5 to 15 hours per month. A moderate Internet user might be online 20 to 50 hours per month. A heavy Internet user might be connected more than 50 hours per month.

Some service providers offer basic dial-up services that have a sliding scale based on the level of use. These types of accounts charge a combination of a flat monthly rate that may include free hours and then an hourly rate. Many service providers offer a flat rate for high-volume accounts. Keep in mind that these charges are separate from any toll charges paid to the telephone company for connecting to the service provider's account. A typical IP account might have a one-time setup charge of $50 to $100 and a monthly charge of $30, which may include several free hours of connect time. After the free hours are used, an hourly rate applies, which is usually less than $2

40

an hour. A high-volume IP account might have a flat monthly charge of around $120 or more. Keep in mind these are only the connection costs charged by the service provider; any telecommunications charges are separate and billed by your local telephone company.

Most service providers get swamped with incoming calls from single IP accounts and other user accounts. It is not unusual to get busy signals over and over again. Many service providers offer a permanent or dedicated port option as a way around this traffic jam. A *dedicated port* is your own private connection that is always available. The dedicated port connection is more expensive, but it guarantees that whenever you dial into the service provider, you'll get connected.

Adding Multiple E-mail Accounts to a Single IP Account

The single IP account is the cheapest connection to the Internet, but this type of account is designed for only one user. This means that it supports only a single private e-mail address. When a single IP account is established, the single-user login name is the e-mail address for that account; for example, *bheslop@bookware.com.* Although the business has the domain name *bookware.com*, by default one user is assigned the e-mail box for that domain name.

For many small businesses with just a few people, the cost of establishing a LAN IP account to support multiple e-mail addresses is an expensive jump from sharing a single-user IP account. Because e-mail is an important business communications tool on the Internet, some service providers let small businesses create multiple e-mail accounts connected to a single-user IP account. Other options are also available, including using an e-mail forwarding service, or establishing a UUCP account. The following sections explain these options for establishing a multiple-user e-mail presence on the Internet with a single-user IP account.

Adding E-mail Boxes through Your Service Provider

The best way to add multiple e-mail boxes to a single IP account is through your service provider. Having individual e-mail boxes for each person working on the Internet is a critical factor for a business. Availability of this service is an important criterion in determining whether you should use the service provider.

Single dial-up IP accounts usually use a POP3 (Post Office Protocol version 3) server for storing and distributing e-mail. A POP3 server stores mail into a specified mailbox (directory) for the single-user IP account. To get your mail, you connect to the POP3 server using an e-mail program, and the mail is sent to the person's local computer. A service provider that offers additional e-mail boxes sets up additional POP3 mailboxes for an additional fee. For example, AlterNet charges $10 a month for each additional POP3 e-mail address. PSI also lets you set up an IP account and purchase another e-mail address for a one-time registration fee of $35 and around $57 dollars a quarter. These e-mail boxes allow several people sharing a single IP account to get mail from their private e-mail boxes. Each user has a login name and e-mail address under the domain name. For example, mail can be sent to *bheslop@bookware.com* and *dangell@bookware.com.* Only one user can be connected at one time, but that user can get only his or her mail. If one person is getting mail, others are not allowed to log on until that person gets his or her mail and disconnects. Each user can have a TCP/IP program on his or her machine, so it's not necessary to share a single computer.

Using Forwarding Services

Some server services offer a low-cost service that lets you use existing e-mail accounts and make it look as though the accounts exist under a unified domain name. This option is useful only if all the people you want to have e-mail addresses under your domain name already have e-mail accounts either with service providers or online services, such as MCI Mail, CompuServe, or America Online. For example, you can have all e-mail that arrives for *bob@bookware.com* sent to Bob's account on CompuServe, and have all mail that arrives for *dave@bookware.com* sent to Dave's MCI Mail account. Figure 3.3 illustrates how a forwarding service works. The e-mail forwarding service also modifies the e-mail address used for outgoing e-mail messages, so messages from the e-mail account appear as if they are coming from within your business domain. To the recipients of your e-mail, the mailbox they sent the message to is the same one you're replying from.

One of the most popular server services for setting up mail forwarding is the Messenger service offered by The Internet Company. If you already have an IP account with your own domain name, you contact the service provider to say you want The Internet Company or other server service to become your new mail server. This requires the service provider to make

FIGURE 3.3
How a forwarding service works

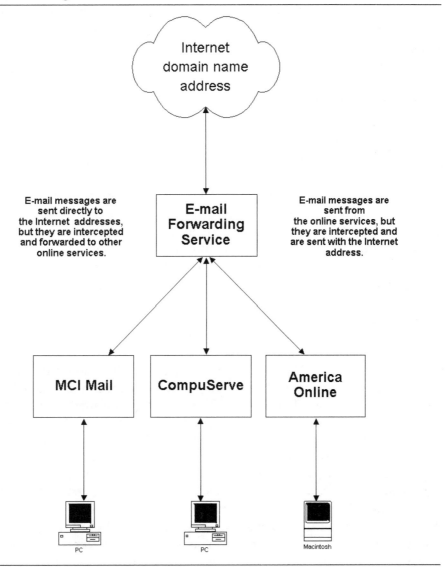

some changes to direct the mail to the server service. Most service providers will work with server services, and most will not charge you for making these changes. If you don't have a domain name, The Internet Company will register the name with the InterNIC on your behalf. After the name is registered, your mail can be sent to the new address. It usually takes a couple of weeks to get your domain name. For a $50 one-time setup fee and a $100 annual maintenance fee, The Internet Company will link up to 10 e-mail addresses under your domain name.

Using a UUCP Mail Account

UUCP offers an affordable solution to establish a domain name and allow several users to receive e-mail on your local LAN separate from your single-user IP account. UUCP (UNIX to UNIX copy) is a batch program set up to periodically check your e-mail (and USENET news) at the service provider's computer at intervals you specify. It dials up the service provider's computer, downloads incoming e-mail, and uploads outgoing e-mail messages. UUCP connections are relatively cheap—$30 to $60 a month. Some service providers, such as Netcom, will tie both a UUCP account to handle e-mail and a single-user IP account to work with the other tools of the Internet under the same domain name.

Setting up a UUCP account is a more demanding solution than getting separate e-mail boxes. Depending on your technical expertise, choosing a UUCP connection may require you to hire a consultant to set up the UUCP connection on your end so that e-mail gets downloaded and routed correctly on your local network. To use a UUCP account for your mail, you must establish a UUCP account with a service provider. When you set up the account with a service provider, the service provider will register your domain name, if you don't already have one connected with an IP account. Internet Anywhere is a commercial Windows UUCP program that is relatively easy to set up on your LAN server. Waffle is a shareware product made for DOS, but it can be used in conjunction with the HellDiver Windows front-end. On the Macintosh side, UUCP/Connect from InterCon is the most popular commercial package. It comes in two versions. The server version lets you distribute mail and news. The client version, called UUCP/Connect LITE, is used on each person's computer to receive e-mail from the UUCP/Connect server. UUCP is built into UNIX.

❑ ESTABLISHING A LAN IP CONNECTION

To connect multiple users on a LAN to the Internet under a single domain name, you have two options: using a router or a UNIX workstation. Either one acts as a gateway between your LAN and the Internet. To connect to the Internet using either of these options, you need a class C IP address and a LAN IP account. You also need a leased digital telecommunications line to handle the data traffic, which is covered later in this chapter. The following section gives an overview of what is involved in getting a LAN IP account, and the UNIX and router options.

Shopping for a LAN IP Account

When it comes to LAN IP accounts, you'd better shop around. Every service provider charges a setup fee, which may include hardware, depending on the type of line you want to use. Setup fees for some major service providers we checked with ranged from $300 to $1,500. All service providers also charge a monthly fee. The monthly fee for the same service providers ranged from $200 to $600. These charges include the cost of the leased line, which is handled by the service provider, although the line is installed by the telephone company.

FYI
See the appendix for a listing of service providers.

Taking the UNIX Gateway Route

For most small businesses running PC or Macintosh networks, the UNIX route is currently prohibitive because setting up and maintaining a UNIX workstation is an expensive and complex process. But because UNIX is the standard multitasking operating system for the Internet, using a UNIX-based system as a gateway to the Internet offers more capabilities. Purchasing a UNIX workstation runs anywhere from $4,000 to $25,000. On top of this, you need someone with UNIX system administration expertise to set up the UNIX workstation and connect it to your existing network. IP consultants can easily cost between $150 and $250 an hour. This is the trickiest variable in figuring the cost of establishing a presence, and spending several thousand dollars for a consultant's services is not unreasonable. To keep your system secure, you probably need additional security to keep incoming Internet users from getting access to any of your sensitive files. Stopping incoming traffic at a location typically requires creating what is known as a *firewall*, which disables some of the packet-sharing network facilities to protect the internal network. Creating a firewall requires a great deal of UNIX and programming knowledge. Some consultants make a good living just from creating firewalls. Expect to pay around $5,000 to secure your network with a firewall.

FYI

As Windows NT becomes more established, PC-based companies will be able to use this multitasking operating system to create gateways to the Internet and establish Internet servers instead of having to use UNIX workstations. Additionally, Apple distributes a version of UNIX (A/UX) and will eventually introduce a multitasking Macintosh operating system with TCP/IP built in.

Going the Router Route

Because introducing a UNIX server is a complex task for most businesses based on DOS/Windows and Macintosh networks, using a router is a more affordable and easier route to take. A router is a hardware box connected to a host on the LAN. The router typically has built-in PPP or SLIP support. It acts as a gateway for the computers on the LAN that the router is connected to. To use the router, each computer on the network must run a TCP/IP program. The router gets the information packets and routes the packets to the individual users on the network. Each packet has addressing information and the information needed to reassemble the complete file at its destination. The router reads the address information and uses its internal routing tables to determine which path to take to deliver the information to the right person on the network. You have to assign the router port the IP address for the network, which will act as a gateway and give each computer its own IP address. Using a router tied to a network, you can easily let 2 to 200 users access the Internet, depending on the capacity of your telecommunications line.

Routers offer features other than just routing packets. They also let you set up ways of securing your network and let you track of activities on your network. You can set up your router to poll your service provider; for example, to retrieve your company's e-mail. Keep in mind that there are different types of routers. For example, some routers include a modem, and others are made specifically for ISDN. Plan to pay around $1,000 and up for a router.

Make sure the service provider you want to use supports the router you want to use. Otherwise, you could spend days trying to configure a router that your service provider does not support. Some companies offer PPP software that can turn a computer with a 386 or higher processor into a dedicated router. Some service providers, such as PSI, offer package deals offering the router, connection, and technical support over the phone for setting up the router. To work on the Internet, the router must meet RFC 1294 requirements for routers. Some of the most popular router vendors are Cisco, Livingston, Telebit, MorningStar, and Ascend. See the appendix for more information on router vendors and products, under "Connection Hardware."

❏ THE TELECOMMUNICATIONS FACTOR

Finding an economical way to connect to a service provider is a major factor in getting your business wired to the Internet. Telecommunications costs— from the basic voice-grade telephone lines to the high-volume digital lines— can be expensive. It's important to estimate the amount of data traffic your connection is going to need in determining the true cost of your Internet connection. The term *bandwidth* refers to the amount of data traffic handled by any connection. Generally, the more bandwidth you require, the more expensive the line. The more bandwidth supported by a given line, the more users can work on the Internet at one time. The two types of telecommunication lines are *analog* or voice and *digital*. Leased lines are almost always digital. At the low end of the bandwidth spectrum are voice lines that typically support a single-user IP account. Your business may need the higher bandwidth offered by digital lines, ISDN or leased. Digital lines offer increased bandwidth as well as improved reliability of the service. AT&T estimates a voice line has a reliability rate of 75 percent, a digital line, 99 percent.

Project your telecommunication costs carefully before you establish an IP account. You must anticipate the bandwidth you need as well as the amount of time your business will be connected to your service provider before you can accurately determine your telecommunications costs. For example, if you're using standard voice-grade telephone lines or ISDN service from your local telephone company, you need to check with your local telephone company to calculate your costs. In most cases, you will be charged a measured unit for business calls made within a certain radius. If your service provider's access number is within the local calling area, your telephone charges will be manageable if you're not connected for a long time every day. If the telephone access number of the service provider is outside the local area, your telephone charges become an important factor and may make the difference between whether it is cost-effective to use POTS, ISDN, or a leased line.

Working with POTS

The lowest level of bandwidth connection is plain old telephone service, referred to as *POTS*. This is the voice-grade analog telephone line commonly used everywhere. These lines are best suited for low-volume IP accounts. The language of computers is digital, so computers communicating with each other over POTS lines must use modems to translate digital to analog and back again. The modem factor in determining your connection charges is explained in the next section.

In most areas of the United States, business telephone services charge tolls for calls that connect you to a service provider's local number. These message-unit charges vary depending on the number you're calling. If you're operating a business out of a residence, however, the telephone service is usually considered residential and typically includes unlimited message units within a local calling area. If you have employees that are telecommuting and working at home, and the service provider has an access number within your local calling area, you won't have telephone toll charges beyond the basic residential rate. But for businesses located at business sites, this is not an option. Be aware that the local telephone charges can add up for a business connecting to a service provider over standard dial-up voice lines.

Most large service providers have POP facilities that let customers connect to their service using a local access number from major metropolitan areas. A POP, which stands for *point of presence*, is a facility leased from telephone companies that provides access to the service provider. This means that even though the service provider's site is thousands of miles away, with a local POP you can use a local number to connect to the service provider.

Some service providers offer an 800 telephone number for access but add a surcharge to their hourly charges. Although it is more expensive than using a local access number, 800 number service can save money if you're using your IP account on the road. Calls made on telephone credit cards can get expensive.

An older system that can be used to lower the telecommunications costs for accessing a service provider are public data networks (PDN). Whereas a POP connection lets you log in directly to your service provider's network, a PDN handles volume telecommunications at cheaper rates than regular telephone companies. The PDN rates vary depending on the time you're calling and from where you're calling. In many cases, you won't need to have your own PDN account because service providers provide the service and add the charges to your account. If you're connecting to a service provider that doesn't offer its own POP or PDN facilities, however, you may want to set up your own PDN account. Keep in mind that having your own PDN account may involve an extra step: having to dial and log into the PDN to connect to your service provider.

The Modem Speed Factor

Modems are the number one access route for most single-user IP accounts. The speed of a modem has a direct bearing on your connection charges, both for the telephone company charges and the service provider's connection charges. The faster your modem connection, the faster you can download and upload information between the host's computer and yours. The less connection time, the less you're charged.

For IP accounts, you should use at least a 9600 bps, 14.4 kbps, or 28.8 kbps modem. However, a modem can transfer information only as fast as the modem it's connected to at the service provider. Many service providers use the slower 9600 bps modems for IP accounts that dial up to nondedicated ports. If you connect a 14.4 kbps modem to a 9600 modem to transfer files, you are going to be working at 9600 bps, not 14.4 kbps. Before establishing a dial-up IP account, check with your prospective service providers about the modem speeds they support.

When you're dealing with telephone charges and hourly connection charges for IP accounts, time is money. The faster the modem, the quicker you do your work and get off. The following shows the different times to transfer a file at different modem speeds. A fast modem can quickly add up to big savings.

Modem Speed	Transfer Time
2,400 bps	14.5 minutes
9,600 bps	3.3 minutes
14,400 bps	2.2 minutes

There are a variety of modem protocol standards. Currently, the fastest international standard is V.32bis, but modem protocols quickly change. V.Fast is the next upcoming standard. The term *bis*, by the way, is French for the second item in a series, so the V.42bis is an extension of the V.42 protocol. We used the US Robotics Courier/V.42bis and Intel 144/144e throughout this project on our PCs. We used a TelePort Mercury 19.2 kbps modem from Global Village on the Macintosh side. The V.Fast sets a standard transfer speed of 28,800 bits per second. For more information on modem vendors, see the appendix under "Connection Hardware."

Beyond having a fast modem, make sure your PC can handle the high speed of incoming data. If you're using a PC, you can improve your chances of reliable communications at speeds over 9600 bps by replacing the Intel 8250 chip in your serial port with the 16550AF chip. If you're using a 386 or later, chances are you don't have to worry about this chip.

Catching the ISDN Wave

ISDN, which stands for Integrated Services Digital Network, is a new type of telecommunications service now being offered to telephone company business and residential customers in many areas. ISDN's low cost, digital connectivity, higher bandwidth, and fast setup makes it an economical solution for connecting small LANs to the Internet. Each ISDN line includes two digital 64 kbps channels, called *bearer* channels (B-channels for short) that can be combined for 128 kbps throughput. The location of the phone company's office determines if you will be able to get 64 kbps or 56 kbps per channel. If you are within a certain distance from the central office that provides the ISDN service, you will enjoy 64 kbps speeds. Your throughput also depends on the hardware and software you are using to support the ISDN. If you use a serial connection, you will be limited to 38.4 kbps. Some service providers use only one channel to connect to the Internet, so you can get only 64 kbps or 56 kbps from the single line. You can also divide the ISDN BRI (basic rate interface) connection to have a channel for your Internet connection and a channel for voice, but this leaves you with a single 64 kbps or 56 kbps connection, depending on your location. If you do this, you also need a special converter to convert the digital signal to an analog signal. Figure 3.4 shows a network connected to a service provider using an ISDN line.

FIGURE 3.4

A network connected to a service provider using an ISDN line

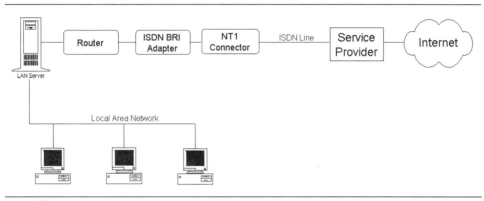

A growing number of metropolitan areas offer ISDN. Most U.S. telephone companies expect ISDN to be 85 percent to 95 percent deployed by 1995. You can call (800) 992–4736 to find out if ISDN is available in your area code. But even if the phone company lists your area, you still need to make sure the service is within a certain distance from the main POP site.

When we checked on ISDN for our area, Silicon Valley, we found an initial fee of $70.75 to get the line installed and a monthly charge of $28. We also found the telephone company bills ISDN lines as measured business lines. The charge for usage was 8 cents for the first minute and 2 cents for each additional minute, provided the POP was within a 12-mile radius from the place of business. With two channels in a single ISDN line, this is double the amount of a regular business rate. The performance of the line depends on the service provider's POP number. If you don't live close to the POP, not only will you have to pay more for the service, but you'll also lose performance of the line. For example, each line on an ISDN connection might supply only 56 kbps, so you get a total of only 112 kbps throughput instead of 128 kbps.

Because ISDN is billed as measured units for local calling, you might find it cheaper to go with a 56 kbps leased line. The trade-off is you get more bandwidth from an ISDN line, but your telephone company charges can get expensive if you are connected for long periods of time. If your business will be a moderate Internet user, between 1 and 4 hours a day, ISDN might be just the answer you're looking for. For example, if you kept your connection active 4 hours a day at 2 cents a minute, the connection cost would be $4.80 a day. For 20 days a month, the cost of the ISDN line would be $96 a month for the line cost. To that, add the service provider's monthly service fee, which can range from $30 to $150. Compare this with the typical cost of a 56 kbps leased line, which can run around $400 a month.

As with any digital line, various hardware expenses are needed to establish an ISDN line, including the following:

- An ISDN interface card (terminal adapter) or router can run from $500 to $1,200. For example, IBM's WaveRunner card supports a digital signal and analog high-speed connections for approximately $600. Hayes also has a interface for the PC (approximately $500), and the Planet ISDN card is available for the Macintosh.

- An ISDN BRI (basic rate interface) line is the actual phone line you typically have installed by your telephone company.

- An NT1 interface is an external box about the size of an external modem. It can cost anywhere from $200 to $400. One is available from Northern Telecom.

- A router that can work with an ISDN connection. For example, PSI and InterNex bundle the Ascend Pipeline 50 with their LAN ISDN connections. Ascend Pipeline 50 routers are available separately for approximately $1,500. The routers support both ISDN and IP (Internet Protocol) routing over dedicated or dial-up digital and analog circuits and include an NT1 interface.

- If you want to use the second channel for voice, you need a special converter (demodulator) that includes a CODEC chip, ISDN phones are available for under $500.

Leasing a Line

Service providers work with the phone company to offer leased lines. For a leased line, your business is charged a flat rate for a larger bandwidth, regardless of the amount of time you're connected. The flat rate of the leased line may seem high at first, but depending on the volume of traffic and the time you are connected, a leased line may be a sound business decision. Digital leased lines are available at speeds of 19.2 kbps, 28.8 kbps, 56 kbps, 128 kbps, T1 (1.544 Mbps) and T3 (4.5 Mbps). Most businesses that are leasing digital lines are using 19.2 kbps, 28.8 kbps, 56 kbps, and 128 kbps bandwidths.

FYI

A switched-56 line is an early digital line offering that used the same infrastructure as POTS. This older technology was a kind of hybrid between analog and digital. Telephone companies are rapidly moving away from this service because of its high expense to operate compared to new digital lines.

Typically, the service provider sets up the leased line with the phone company and charges you a flat fee. This lets you rely on your service provider to solve any line problems with the phone company. When you set up a leased line, the service provider also charges a setup fee. The setup fee varies depending on whether hardware is included. The hardware includes devices that work at both ends of the connection, usually a router and CSU/DSU box (a special digital modem). CSU/DSU stands for customer service unit/data service unit. The CSU/DSU and router handle the traffic between your computer and the Internet. The CSU/DSU typically runs around $500 for 56 kbps. Figure 3.5 shows a network connected to a service provider using a dedicated line.

It is difficult to compare the prices of leased lines because there are so many different pricing structures. The following questions will help you work with service providers when shopping for a leased line.

FIGURE 3.5

A network connected to a service provider using a dedicated line

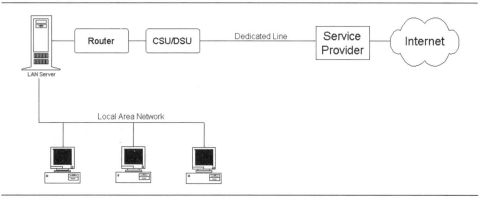

- Who is responsible for working with the phone company to have the line installed?

- How much is the setup fee?

- Does the price depend on the location of your service provider's nearest POP (point of presence)? If so, are the prices for the phone line based on the distance from the POP to your location?

- How much will you be charged for the equipment, and who ends up with the equipment if the service is ended?

- Is the price of equipment higher if purchased from the service provider?

- Are you being charged for the IP account separately from the leased line?

- Are there any additional charges, such as a charge for a dedicated port?

- Does the service provider charge a higher fee for the first 6 months to cover the charge of the equipment, with a lower fee after the first 6 months?

Cabling Your Connection

Cable TV (CATV) looms on the horizon as a high-speed, low-cost Internet connection option. These cables will be capable of 10 Mbps connections, which dwarfs today's T1 connection speeds of about 1.5 Mbps. Although 10 Mbps sounds enticing, keep in mind that many server sites on the Internet are connected at 56 kbps. As a result, unless you're accessing resources located at the provider's site or another cable site, you will experience bottlenecks. Also keep in mind that you will be sharing the 10 Mbps bandwidth with other computer users, and few computers can transfer data over Ethernet at 10 Mbps on a sustained basis.

Currently, only a few service providers are promising or offering CATV service. For example, Hybrid Networks is providing Internet connections to cable TV subscribers in Cupertino, California, for about $100 a month. The connection operates at 10 Mbps for incoming traffic, but only at modem speeds for outgoing traffic. The service requires a computer with an Ethernet adapter, a high-speed modem, and a remote link adapter that supports DES encryption and costs around $1,500.

❏ SHOPPING FOR THE RIGHT SERVICE PROVIDER

We would like to direct you to the perfect service provider, but one solution doesn't exist. Instead, you need to find out what is available in your area that meets your needs. Ask yourself what services your company needs. Setting up an IP account correctly can save you time later. Choosing a service provider requires some thought as to your needs and costs. Here are some things to keep in mind when shopping for a service provider.

- What type of IP accounts does the service provider offer? Be sure the service provider can accommodate your current and future account needs. For example, can you change from a single dial-up IP account to a LAN IP account that connects to the service provider using a router?

- What are the sign-up charges? Most service providers charge a one-time sign-up fee.

- What is the basic monthly service charge? Most providers charge a basic monthly fee; some charge a minimum fee plus usage.

- What are the hourly connection charges for the service? Don't confuse this charge with telecommunications charges, which are often billed in addition to the hourly service charge. Some service providers charge different hourly rates for busy times versus off times, and others use a flat hourly rate regardless of the time. Some service providers don't charge by the hour, but charge a flat rate.

- How much storage space are you allotted for files and e-mail? Many service providers charge you for disk space beyond a minimum amount allotted for your account.

- What modem speeds are you and the service provider using? Some service providers charge different hourly rates depending on the modem speed you're using. For example, a 9600 bps modem has a cheaper hourly rate than a 14.4 kbps modem, but it may cost you more in telecommunications charges because it takes longer to download a file to your computer.

- Does the service provider provide technical and customer support either via e-mail or over the telephone?

- Will the service provider help you set up a router or CSU/DSU box?

- Are there any additional charges for adding people to your class C IP address to give them access to the Internet?

- Ask for references. In some cases, a service provider will give you a company name that has set up a business similar to yours.

- Where is the service provider located, and what POPs are available?

- Can you call more than one number if the host computer is congested?

- Does the service provider also have a toll-free number or network of POPs for connecting when you are on a business trip?

- Does the provider use static or dynamic addressing? (See the glossary for definitions of these terms.)

- Does the service provider offer a dedicated port option?

- Does your service provider require you to purchase any additional equipment for your connection?

- Does the service provider offer any equipment as a part of a package deal?

- Are there any hidden costs?

Information You Need to Set Up an IP Account

Once you have determined the type of account and services you want, you need to get some information to set up your account. Even if you don't need all of the following information to set up the SLIP/PPP account, it is a good idea to have on hand in case another program requires it.

- Your assigned host name

- Your registered domain name

- Your IP address

- Your subnet mask number

- The phone numbers that are available for your area for the speed modem you are using

- The name and address of the e-mail SMTP (Simple Mail Transfer Protocol) server.

- The name and address of the network news NNTP (Network News Transport Protocol) server

- The name and address of the service provider's domain name server (DNS)

Chapter 4

□ □ □

Setting Up Shop on the Internet

After getting your business connected to the Internet, the next step toward establishing your business presence on the Internet is to set up a server presence. Working with the server side of e-mail, FTP, Gopher, and World-Wide Web lets users interact with your business in all kinds of exciting ways. You can send out requested information automatically via e-mail, publish information online, or operate a virtual storefront to do business on the Internet. This chapter explains the fundamentals of establishing and promoting a server presence on the Internet.

□ THE TWO SERVER PATHS YOU CAN TAKE

You have two ways to establish a server presence on the Internet: doing it yourself, where you set up and maintain the server at your business site, or setting up a server presence for your business using a server service. Setting up a server at your site requires you to have the communications connection and the computing resources to support incoming Internet traffic at your end of the IP connection. The following sections explain and compare the do-it-yourself server option and the server-service option.

The Do-It-Yourself UNIX Server Approach

The do-it-yourself server approach requires a UNIX server, a dedicated connection, a leased, high-volume data transmission line for handling incoming traffic, and technical expertise to put it all together. The standard multitasking operating system for the Internet is UNIX, which has built-in TCP/IP support. Without a multitasking operating system, it's not feasible to have dedicated connection with several Internet users working on your server at the same time.

A UNIX system can act as your gateway to the Internet as well as your server presence. But the UNIX route to establishing a server presence is not cheap, as you learned in Chapter 3 in the section on "Taking the UNIX Gateway Route": $4,000 to $25,000 for a UNIX computer, several thousand dollars for a consultant to set up and manage your server, and $5,000 for a firewall (if security is a concern). In addition, to handle a reasonable volume of Internet users connecting to your server requires a dedicated connection and a leased line to handle the data traffic. The price of the leased line depends on the volume of data traffic the line can handle and on your service provider's nearest POP (point of presence) location. Figure on around $500 to install a 56 kbps leased line with a monthly charge of $250. This price varies, since the charge is typically based on the distance from the POP to your location. Additionally, service providers usually charge a setup fee around $1,000 and a monthly charge of around $250 for a dedicated connection. The setup fee usually includes access to the Internet and two pieces of hardware: a router and a CSU/DSU box (a digital conversion device). The CSU/DSU and router handle the traffic between your workstation and the Internet. Think of the CSU/DSU as playing the role of a glorified modem. Figure 4.1 shows the major requirements for setting up your UNIX server.

FIGURE 4.1
The major requirements for setting up a server

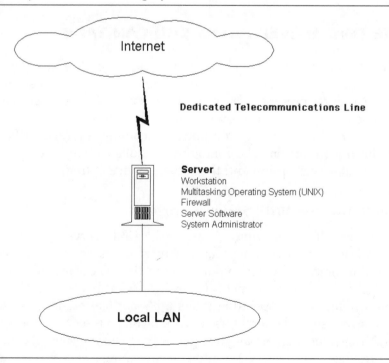

Using Server Services

Because of the complexity and expense of setting up and maintaining a server on your own, a new kind of business service, called server services or service bureaus, has emerged. *Server services* are companies or service providers that set up and maintain servers for businesses by spreading the cost of establishing a server over many businesses. Server services are relatively new, so the types of services, prices, and terms can vary greatly between companies. Server service options are as varied as the tools of the Internet. Costs for server services can range from under few hundred dollars to thousands of dollars.

Server services set up servers that support the tools used by Internet users. For example, a server service could create a World-Wide Web server presence that lets Internet users view online graphic-based information about your products or services. Your server can be part of the server services' electronic mall or a stand-alone site on the Internet. Even businesses with the internal resources to create a server at their site may find the server service a viable option. For example, a marketing department can promote its company via a server and not have to disrupt the in-house MIS department, which may not want to take on the burden of setting up a server or expose the company's network to the outside world.

FYI

See the appendix for a listing of server services.

❏ DESIGNING AND SETTING UP A SERVER PRESENCE

Establishing a server presence involves determining what type of presence you want and what information you want to present, matching the best Internet tool for the job, and shopping for the right server service company. The following sections explain the general process of designing and setting up a server. The specifics involved in creating a server for e-mail, FTP, Gopher, and World-Wide Web are covered in the remainder of the book.

What Your Business Can Do with Servers

You can provide two types of activities using a server: online publishing and virtual storefronts. What you can accomplish using a server depends on the Internet tool or tools you choose to use and your imagination. Different types of servers provide different options for businesses. But one thing they all share is the instant delivery of information and services. Many of your existing business marketing activities can be adapted to work on the Internet. Here are some of the kinds of marketing items that can successfully be translated into Internet server activities:

- Catalogs
- Company background information
- Company contracts
- Customer service information and functions
- Customer support
- Demos
- Dialogs with customers and others
- Documentation and manuals
- Free software
- Job placement or recruitment notices
- Lists of events
- Market or customer surveys
- Pricing information
- Product announcements
- Product specification sheets and performance data
- Promotional notices of specials and sales
- Reviews and product commentary
- Service evaluations

Tool-based Server Options

Four Internet tools define your business service presence on the Internet: e-mail, FTP, Gopher, and World-Wide Web. Each tool offers different advantages and disadvantages for different tasks. Your business can use a combination of these tools to put together an integrated Internet presence that targets different users on the Internet. For example, you might create an e-mail server to send information on demand via e-mail, as well as a World-

Wide Web server to provide a multimedia brochure or catalog. The following explains the key server presence options available to businesses.

- An e-mail server provides information on demand via e-mail to let Internet users—as well as millions more connected to online services that have e-mail gateways to the Internet—get information. Using a mail robot server (called a *mailbot*), any person with an e-mail address can send an e-mail message and receive requested information, such as an announcement or a newsletter. Using a mailing-list service, called a LISTSERV, you can send updates to Internet users that subscribe to the LISTSERV. For more information, see Chapter 5.

- An FTP server is one of the easiest and most useful ways to distribute information in file form. You can create an anonymous FTP server to make files available to anyone on the Internet, or you can create a private FTP server to move files only between people connected to your company. For more information, see Chapter 7.

- A Gopher server lets your business publish information or run a virtual storefront. Because Gopher incorporates powerful search and retrieval capabilities, Internet users can find any Gopher site easily. They can read information online and download files from your Gopher site. Gopher is built around delivering information in text and files. You can create catalogs and store them in files using different formats, such as PostScript, for Internet users to view and print on their local computers. Figure 4.2 shows the first view of a Gopher storefront, and Figure 4.3 shows a Gopher catalog listing. For more information, see Chapter 8.

- The World-Wide Web is the newest and fastest-growing Internet tool, and it promises to be the leading tool for establishing a business presence. A Web server presence offers the most exciting way to publish information or run a virtual storefront on the Internet. Figure 4.4 shows the first view of a World-Wide Web storefront, and Figures 4.5 and 4.6 show additional views. The Web lets users work within a rich environment of hypertext links, graphics, fonts, sound, and video. Internet users use a World-Wide Web client browser, such as Mosaic, to view Web documents. The information from a Web server is brought to the user's computer and presented in the computer's native graphical environment. For more information, see Chapter 9.

FIGURE 4.2

The first view of a Gopher storefront

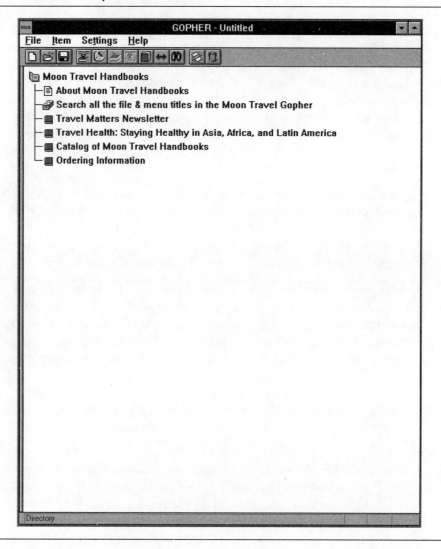

FIGURE 4.3

A Gopher catalog listing

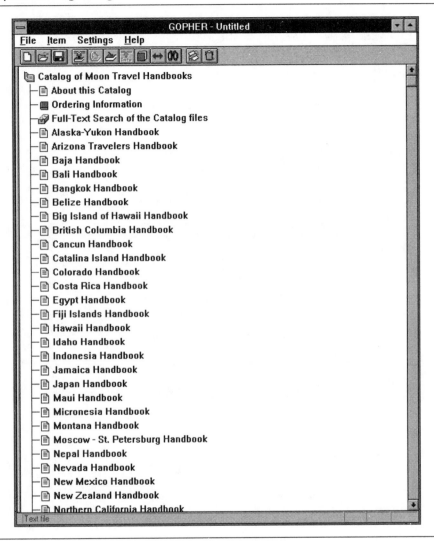

FIGURE 4.4

The first view of a World-Wide Web storefront

FIGURE 4.5
Another screen of the Web storefront

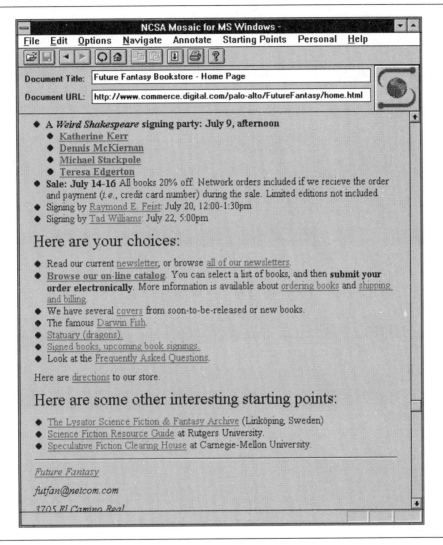

FIGURE 4.6

A catalog browser system in a Web storefront

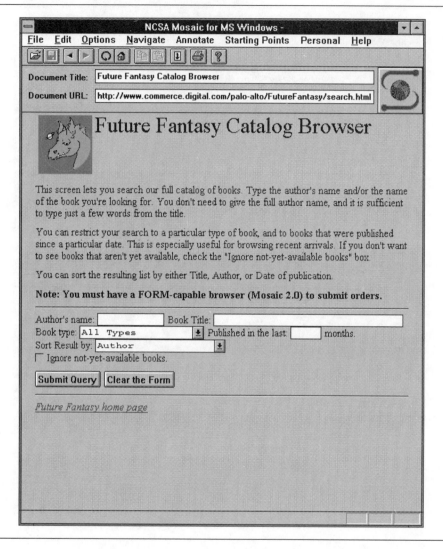

Making Your Server an Attraction

One of the key elements of establishing a server presence is to create a server that attracts Internet users. As you develop your server presence, you need to think about making it a newsworthy attraction, as well as offer incentives to customers to keep them coming back. You have many options for promoting your server if your server offers the Internet community value-added services. Information-rich, content-based information is the rule of the Internet. Package your server presence to offer a resource to people. You want to grab the customer's attention, but remember your server is the only way some people will be exposed to your company. Your server presence is your business. If you step over the legal boundaries, such as including libelous statements or publishing copyrighted or trademarked material, you will lose potential customers and possibly incur legal problems.

FYI

See the end of Chapter 1 for some comments on content-based interactive marketing on the Internet.

Designing Your Server Presence

Establishing a server presence involves determining how to meet your business objectives, deciding what information you want to provide, and designing the structure of the information you want to present on your server. Different tools use different processes to establish a server presence. Keep the following general guidelines in mind when designing your server presence.

- Start out small to get a feel for establishing a presence on the Internet. As you become more comfortable with doing business on the Internet, you can gradually build up your presence to a full-service storefront.

- Take responsibility for defining your role and the server service's role in designing a server presence. Determine what information you want to provide and how you want it to be presented. For example, you need a basic knowledge of Internet tools and their capabilities, and you need to choose the information you want to present. This will save time for the server service and in turn save you money.

- Match your presence with the right tool. Different tools have different access rates. For example, e-mail has the largest distribution. The World-Wide Web can be accessed only by users with IP connections. In many cases, you may integrate multiple servers to present a unified server presence. For example, you might establish an FTP and World-Wide Web server along with a mailbot presence.

- Develop as complete a project plan as possible. Know what you want from the server service. Even if the server service makes different recommendations, you will at least know enough about the project to assess those new ideas. If you want to consider the project in several steps, list each step.

- Consider what connections you want to make between servers. For example, you can have a Gopher server use information stored on your FTP server.

- Be aware of new developments in tools and services.

Working with Server Services

Using a server service to establish your server presence on the Internet is usually cheaper than doing it yourself for most small businesses. However, you need to be an educated consumer of server services to make a sound business decision. You need to understand each tool's server features and capabilities as well as the costs involved in setting up the server. The following are some guidelines to help you become a savvy buyer of server services.

- Determine what you can afford. Develop a budget to keep your server presence running for a minimum period of time.

- Shop around. Server services are popping up everywhere, and the pricing of services is always changing. Call server services to get quotes based on what you want. Most server services will provide some free consultations to establish the project and your costs. If you have more than one consultant providing quotes, you can compare the cost and time estimates. Try to get any sales literature that service services offer. Many of these businesses don't produce the standard brochures used in everyday business, but they may have set up mailbots to distribute information on services and pricing.

- Determine the costs associated with the type of server presence you want. Many server services charge a basic setup fee, monthly fee, and additional fees, depending on the type of server and what you want to do. For example, if you want to take credit-card orders, some server services charge for each transaction. Be sure to calculate the costs for every aspect of setting up the site. For example, include costs of designing and creating the Web documents, storage costs, credit-card transaction charges, download charges, and any consulting charges.

- Ask for a proposal defining the job, the proposed solution, and the estimated time frame to establish the server presence. Be sure the proposal includes the specific services the server service will provide and lists what the server service expects from you. The costs of each part of the project can vary because some server services work on a hourly rate and others bid by the job. Keep in mind that often many variables are involved in establishing a server presence, so you need to define all the costs.

- Negotiate, negotiate, negotiate. Setting up a presence on the Internet using the services of a server service requires negotiating a package. Published prices are not any more binding than rate cards are for advertising. Don't assume that a proposal is a final offer. You may have room to negotiate every item in the proposal. Consider the proposal a working document from which to start negotiating. Concentrate your negotiations on those areas where you will save the most money. You can easily spend more time than it's worth to rework a proposal. On the other hand, you may be able to spend just a few minutes and save hundreds of dollars.

- Don't judge by price alone; check out different server service sites using the tools that you are considering for establishing a presence. For example, use a Gopher client, such as WinGopher, to view Gopher sites and a World-Wide Web browser, such as Mosaic, to view World-Wide Web sites. Seeing is believing. Compare the different sites to see which ones do the best job at presenting information from different companies.

- Find out how you will deliver documents to the server service to post on your server. For example, can you upload a file to its system, or do you have to send hard copy with a disk? Can you update the documents yourself, or does the server service do it for you? If the server service does it for you, ask how much it charges.

- Ask what format the server service requires. Some server services let you submit a file in your word processor's format; others require you to convert the file to a specific format. Some service providers let you submit documents in your word processor's format, but they charge you to convert the file.

- Determine how your company will monitor the results. Find out how the server service tracks activity. Ask for a sample report to see if the information is useful as it's generated. If not, see if you can get a customized report.

- Determine how the server provider is marketing its services on the Internet and in non-Internet publications.

- Inquire about any miscellaneous charges required to support your server. These costs can be substantial and are separate from the basic setup and monthly fees. Fees are charged for such services as setting up your domain name, mail forwarding, document authoring (HTML for Web pages), image scanning, editing, format conversions, extracting data from existing databases files, integrating current services with custom or off-the-shelf search engines, and data updates.

- Do a background check on each server service. Review their site. Check with companies that have established a presence on the server service's server. Ask the server service for references.

- Keep any changes to a minimum. Changes cost money. If either you or the server service needs to change the schedule, make sure everyone agrees.

- Determine a payment schedule at the same time you establish the project timetable. The best payment schedule is to pay one half after the work is completed and the remaining half after 30 days, when you are sure the system works as promised.

- Keep in mind that when you create a server presence using the services of a server service, your server presence is located under its domain name unless you specifically request otherwise. For example, the address for a Gopher server presence for your business at Cyberspace Development's site would be *marketplace.com*, and the address on a Web server at the same site might be *http://www.marketplace.com/bookware/home.html*.

❑ BUILD IT AND THEY WILL COME—IF THEY KNOW ABOUT IT

It's one thing to create a server to deliver services to Internet users, and another thing to let them know it's there. Because the Internet is not controlled or managed by a single organization, getting the word out about your server presence on the Internet takes a concerted, multifaceted campaign. The following sections explain general promotional options available to your business both on and off the Internet to let the world know about your server presence. Promotion options available for specific tools are covered in Chapters 5 to 9.

Promoting Your Server Presence with Traditional Marketing Tools

Every business uses a variety of traditional marketing tools to promote itself, including business cards, display ads, radio spots, and TV commercials. You can use all these traditional marketing tools to promote your server presence to customers already using the Internet. These customers will appreciate knowing about your service—it's a convenience to get information directly to their desktops. Additionally, as more customers use your Internet services, your business can realize substantial savings as you cut back on traditional methods of marketing. For example, sending your newsletter via e-mail saves the printing and postage costs associated with a paper-based newsletter. Here are guidelines for promoting your server presence to your customers.

- Give your customers the options of receiving information, such as a newsletter or new product announcements, automatically via a LISTSERV or mailbot.

- Put your server presence information directly on your business stationery.

- Promote your server presence in your display advertising.

- Include your server presence address in all your direct mailings.

- Create an incentive for customers to continually visit your server presence.

Getting Publicity for Your Server Presence via Paper-Based Media

Getting publicity for your server will increase your visibility on the Internet and give your business credibility. You can publicize your server presence in several ways. A growing number of paper-based publications about the Internet are a good source of free publicity. For example, *Internet World*, *The Internet Letter*, and the *Internet Business Journal* are always looking for new kinds of Internet servers. Don't underestimate the value of promoting your server presence through these publications. These periodicals are frequently quoted in newsgroups and passed on via mailing lists and other Internet users. The amount of publicity your server presence is likely to receive is directly related to the value of it as a resource to the Internet community. As with other forms of promotion dealing with the Internet, center your press information around what your server site is offering as a useful service to the Internet community. For a listing of periodicals, see the "Internet Business Publications" section in the appendix.

Promoting Your Server Presence via the Internet

The Internet provides an increasing number of no-cost options for promoting a server presence. Several useful services will help you get the word out, including LISTSERV mailings, network newsgroups, and various text files that are distributed on the Internet.

The most popular Internet mailing list for announcing new products and services is Net-Happenings. People subscribe to Net-Happenings and receive constant updates via e-mail. To subscribe to Net-Happenings, send an e-mail message that looks like this:

To: listserv@internic.net
Subject: <leave blank>
Skip down to the body of the message and type:
subscribe net-happenings <your name>

Once you subscribe, read different Net-Happenings postings to get an idea of how to structure your announcement. Here are some guidelines for writing an announcement for Net-Happenings:

- Keep announcements short—no longer than two screens or approximately 3,000 characters.

- Limit your announcement to a statement of purpose and the scope of your server presence.

- Exclude promotional hype.

- Include contact information, such as phone and fax numbers, and any pertinent e-mail addresses in addition to your server address.

The Internet Mall is a monthly list of available commercial services on the Internet. This listing includes categories, such as books, magazines, music, video, personal items, games, adult toys, computer hardware and software, research services, travel, and so on. There is no charge for getting your server on this list if you qualify. Dave Taylor maintains this listing and is responsible for the specific prose in each listing. You can add your server presence to this list by sending an e-mail message to *taylor@netcom.com*. The criteria for being on this list are that the company must be on the Internet and must have a salable product, and customers must be able to order through the net directly, either by Gopher, WAIS, Web, or e-mail. Excluded from this list are companies involved in Internet access services and contract technical-support operations.

The Media List is a listing of newspapers, magazines, TV stations, and other media outlets that accept electronic submissions from readers and viewers, along with their main e-mail addresses. This file is distributed via Net-Happenings and newsgroups, including *alt.journalism, alt.internet.services*, and *com.misc*. The media breakdown includes Daily Newspapers, Weekly Newspapers, Magazines, News/Media Services, Newsletters, Radio, TV Stations and Networks, and Computer Publications. Adam Gaffin maintains the Media List.

Chapter 5

Using E-mail for Your Business Communications

Electronic mail, commonly called e-mail, is the number one use of the Internet and is rapidly becoming the dominant form of business communications. The Internet mail system not only includes all the millions of Internet users, but also includes virtually every commercial network, including CompuServe, America Online, Delphi, MCI Mail, and others. Tapping into the Internet's e-mail system is a must for establishing a presence on the Internet for your business. This chapter explains the dynamics of effectively establishing, managing, and utilizing a business e-mail presence on the Internet.

❏ WHAT E-MAIL IS AND HOW IT WORKS

E-mail is a powerful communications tool that is simple to use. It's at once instant, intimate, and global in scope. Working with e-mail requires three things:

- Access to the Internet or an online service that has a mail gateway to the Internet
- An e-mail program
- The e-mail address of the person you want to reach

An e-mail address is usually made up of the user name and the host computer used by that user, separated by an @ sign, in the format *username@hostname*. For example, our e-mail addresses are *dangell@bookware.com* and *bheslop@bookware.com*. An e-mail message has two basic parts: the header information and the body of the message. The header contains items such as the sender's name, the subject, and date. The body is the text of an e-mail message. Figures 5.1 and 5.2 show typical e-mail messages created on the PC and Macintosh, respectively.

Common characteristics of e-mail programs are that they let users compose and send e-mail, and then read and organize the e-mail they receive. Mail programs usually list the e-mail messages from an in box, showing the mail message's header information. Figure 5.3 shows a sample listing of messages.

Connection points between e-mail systems or networks are called *gateways.* A gateway acts as a translator to communicate across different e-mail

FIGURE 5.1

An e-mail message created using Chameleon for the PC

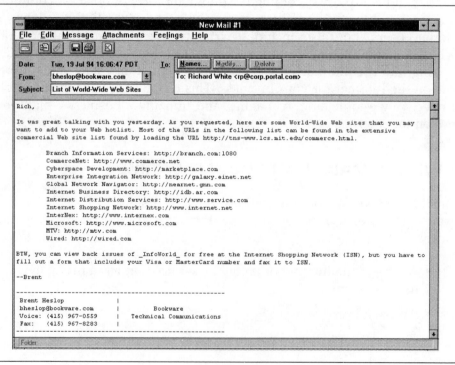

FIGURE 5.2

An e-mail message created using Eudora for the Macintosh

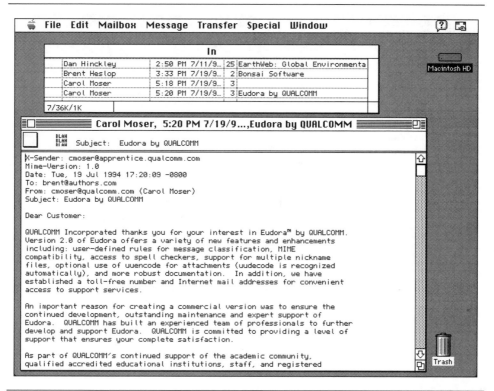

protocols. Shell account users usually use a UNIX-based mail program such as elm, pine, or mail on the service provider's computer. IP account e-mail programs are usually a part of TCP/IP packages. Some e-mail packages offer features beyond the bundled e-mail programs and are sold separately, such as Eudora and SunSelect Mail. Networked companies typically use their internal e-mail programs, such as cc: Mail or WordPerfect Office, and purchase a gateway program to let e-mail be routed to and from the Internet.

Most e-mail programs support the MIME protocol to let Internet users attach nontext files to e-mail messages. MIME, which stands for Multipurpose Internet Mail Extension, lets users send mail in any format, so you can send graphic images, formatted documents, and audio, video, and compressed data files to other Internet users.

FIGURE 5.3

A listing of message headers from a user's e-mail in box

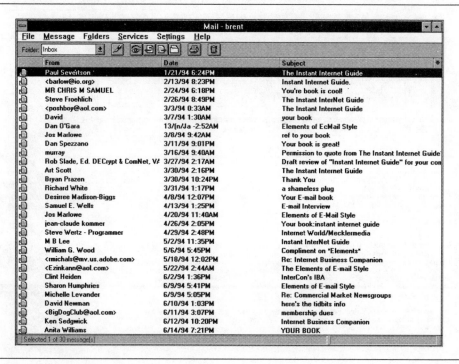

Recognizing the Business Benefits of E-mail

Connecting your business to the Internet's electronic mail system opens up new marketing, collaboration, and efficiency opportunities. E-mail offers the most bang for the buck for conducting business on the Internet. It combines the precision of letters and memos with the immediacy of a phone call. This valuable communications tool is rapidly becoming as important as the telephone or fax. Businesses are recognizing the benefits of e-mail for communicating internally as well as with the outside world. Here are some of the advantages to your business of using e-mail:

- It eliminates phone tag and improves response times.

- It allows you to digest your messages and put more thought into your responses, compared to using the phone.

- It breaks down distance and time barriers of traditional written communications. You can send and read e-mail messages at any time, 24 hours a day, 365 days a year, for better communication across time zones.

- It shortens the cycle of written communication. People can circumvent many of the inefficiencies of the office and the approval process of traditional paper-based communication.

- It empowers the individual by flattening out corporate and sociological hierarchies and allowing for direct, interactive communication.

- It improves productivity by speeding up the decision-making process by providing a forum for replies or clarifications.

- It facilitates meeting planning and preparation.

- It creates flexibility in the workday by reducing telephone interruptions, and it allows people to work from home or any other location with a computer.

- It reduces postal and telephone charges.

Establishing an E-mail Presence on the Internet

Establishing an e-mail presence involves setting up e-mail boxes, which is part of the process of getting your business wired to the Internet, as explained in Chapter 3. These mailboxes let your business communicate with anyone who has an e-mail box accessible from the Internet. On the server side, your business can establish an e-mail server presence. Two types of server presence options are available to businesses: *mailbots* and *mailing lists*. Mailbots let anyone who has an e-mail address and access to the Internet request any document on demand via e-mail by simply requesting it in an e-mail message sent to a mail robot's e-mail address. For example, a customer can send a message to *info@bookware.com* to receive information about our business. A mailing list lets your business distribute information on an ongoing basis to Internet users who subscribe to it, such as sending newsletters or updates. We explain establishing these servers later in this chapter.

❑ MANAGING YOUR BUSINESS
E-MAIL COMMUNICATIONS

Communicating via e-mail outside your business is a convenient, instant communications medium, but it can easily become an overwhelming and cluttered medium that demands tending beyond what is reasonable. You need to manage your e-mail connection to ensure it's a productivity tool and not a time-consuming quagmire. Think carefully about what kind of e-mail you want to handle and for what reason before you start to promote your e-mail presence. The following sections provide general guidelines for establishing and managing your business e-mail communications.

Managing Your Incoming E-mail

Managing incoming e-mail is critical to the success of your Internet business presence. Before you start promoting e-mail addresses to customers, vendors, and others, you need to plan how to handle the flow of e-mail in your business. To help your business sort and direct incoming e-mail, most e-mail programs have incorporated agents, commonly referred to as filters and rules, to automatically sift through and sort incoming messages. An *agent* is a broad term for any automated process that performs a desired action with little or no human intervention. A *filter* is a class of agent that can sort through your messages. *Rules* are the criteria that you define, such as searching for a specific user's name or text.

Using filters and rules, you can identify specific information in the header of a message and redirect the message to a specific folder, forward the message, or execute other commands on the message. All mail programs support *folders*, which are special storage holders for mail messages. How you use folders depends on the mail program you're using. For example, you can set up your mail program to deliver e-mail to your sales department by creating a folder that receives e-mail addressed to *orders@ bookware.com*. This way, you can track all incoming orders and not risk losing an order among your personal messages. Figure 5.4 illustrates how messages can be sent to specific folders using rules.

Filters can be especially valuable if you have someone who, for whatever reason, decides to mail-bomb you. *Mail bombing* means that someone bombards you with a steady stream of flaming e-mail messages. A *bozo filter* is simply a filter that searches for mail from a specific individual. In essence, a bozo filter lets you reserve the right not to deal with the person by filtering any mail sent from the person. You can either direct the mail bomb to a

FIGURE 5.4

Rules can organize your messages by routing them to specific folders

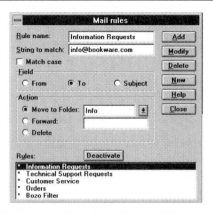

special folder or execute a command to automatically delete the mail from the e-mail terrorist.

You can also use filters for promotions. For example, you might want to publicize an e-mail drawing in a newsletter using an address, such as *promo@wkrp.com*. The filter can be set up to look for a specific message that contains a phrase such as *free ticket drawing* in the subject line. You can then set up a filter to sort messages in response to the announcement and give away the prize to, say, the tenth person sending an e-mail message containing the phrase.

Broadcasting an E-mail Message

Make sure the recipients of your e-mail broadcasts want to get the information you are sending. Unsolicited or junk e-mail is frowned upon by most Internet users. The consequences of sending unsolicited e-mail are quite different from sending out traditional junk mail via the U.S. Postal Service. E-mail is a more interactive medium than traditional mail. If a person feels you are sending junk e-mail, he or she may flame you or mail-bomb you. For this reason, we recommend that you use only the mailing list you create from your customer base. The keyword here is *unsolicited*, so it is fine to communicate with people who have provided your business with their e-mail addresses for the purpose of receiving specific information via e-mail.

When you create any e-mail message for broadcasting to a group, don't use traditional advertising copy. The Internet community is content-oriented and wants quality, filtered information. Couch your message within a commentary that is applicable to the Internet audience. Nothing is more obvious in ASCII text than empty hype.

Keep in mind that people who communicate with electronic mail expect a faster response from you than with traditional letters. Providing customer support via e-mail messages needs to be managed and channeled to the right people in your business. Making sure that a message doesn't get lost and is processed in a timely manner is key to providing customer support.

Using a Signature File as Your E-mail Letterhead

Every e-mail program lets you create a special signature file. A *signature* file is a text file that contains additional information about an individual or business and is automatically appended to the end of an outgoing message. Signature files can contain information that would be included in a standard letterhead, such as your business name, postal address, fax number, other e-mail addresses, and so on. You can add any kind of information you want. Just as you promote your company with a logo on paper stationery, your e-mail signature is an excellent place to promote your business. The following is a sample signature advertising Bookware:

```
================================================================
Brent Heslop                  |
bheslop@bookware.com          |         Bookware
Voice: (415) 967–0559         |    Technical Communications
Fax: (415) 967–8283           |

================================================================
```

Creating Aliases to E-mail Groups

Most e-mail programs support aliases or nicknames. An *alias* is a single name that references a group mailing list. This is great tool for routing mail messages to any group of people. Using aliases is a real time-saver for creating specialized mailings. For example, if you want all your customers who have purchased a particular product or service from you to be informed of a new related product, you can create an alias to send the information to only those customers. Figure 5.5 shows how you can use aliases to direct mail to specific individuals.

FIGURE 5.5
An alias lets you direct mail to specific individuals

You can also use aliases to define a user. For example, say one person receives e-mail for two different addresses. For example, *bob@bookware.com* could also receive mail at *support@bookware.com* and *info@bookware.com*. The message identifies the type of action Bob needs to take to handle the message.

Almost all e-mail programs let you create aliases that let you store a group of e-mail addresses to do a broadcast mailing. Using an alias, you can mail a newsletter to a large of group of people who have stated they want to be on your electronic mailing list. As explained later in this chapter, you or a server service can use a mailing-list server to create an automatic system for collecting e-mail addresses and sending out e-mail messages, such as newsletters and other documents. It may seem simple to create an alias of all the people you want to receive your newsletter or be sent your mailing. In theory this is great, but most service providers and different mail programs have different capabilities and settings that affect how many people can exist in an alias. For example, you may find that your service provider allows you to create an alias of only 75 names. The answer is to set up several aliases or use a mailing-list server.

Forwarding E-mail

One of the most common ways to direct mail messages is forwarding. Forwarding sends a mail message from one user to another. Like call forwarding, e-mail forwarding routes your e-mail to another address. If one

83

person is in charge of orders and is going on vacation, you can use forwarding to send the e-mail to another person. In most cases, when you work with a server service any inquiries or messages are forwarded to your e-mail address.

Depending on the features of the mail program you're using, you may be able to create a mailbot using the vacation mail feature of your mail client. A mail program's vacation feature is normally used to notify users that send e-mail to an account that the person is on vacation or not available to read your message. If you simply change the message indicating you're away to a different message, a simple mail account becomes an inexpensive mail server. Incoming mail that is addressed to *info@bookware.com* would be placed in a separate folder and the vacation reply sent automatically from that folder.

Some e-mail programs that support filters and rules let you enter commands to process e-mail. If your e-mail program supports this feature, you may be able to create a mailbot that automatically replies to mail sent to a specific address, such as *support@bookware.com*. Keep in mind that unless you have a dedicated connection, the mail will be filtered and the automatic response sent only when you retrieve your mail.

Monitoring Employees' E-mail Usage

The 1986 Electronic Communications Privacy Act prohibits phone- and data-line taps with two exceptions: law-enforcement agencies and *employers.* This act considers internal e-mail to be the property of the company because the company pays for the e-mail system. Therefore, companies have the right to search their company mailboxes. Results of a survey in *MacWorld* magazine (July 1993) stated that 41 percent of the respondents electronically eavesdropped on employees, and nearly two-thirds of management surveyed said there were reasons to eavesdrop on electronic communications.

Although companies have the right to monitor e-mail, it is important to establish an e-mail policy that your employees understand. It is best to establish a policy that respects the e-mail confidentiality of others. Even if you are paying for an employee's mailbox, it is important that you ask for permission before forwarding, inserting, or posting an employee's e-mail message that might cause embarrassment or confidentiality problems.

Protecting Your Business against Internal E-mail Abuse

It's a good idea to establish a company policy against employees leaving a computer unattended, so that one person's e-mail program can't be used by another person. If an unauthorized person gets access to an e-mail account at your business, worse things can happen than just having messages looked at, modified, or deleted. A person can use your business's e-mail account to send or post offensive messages throughout the Internet. The results can be devastating. Most e-mail systems let you lock your screen or your mail program to prevent anyone from using your system. Unlocking the screen or program requires entering the user's password.

Conducting Business Transactions via E-mail

The perception exists that giving out your credit-card number over the Internet is a high risk. Your credit card will be stored in backups and be available to system administrators and possibly other users. But think about this for a moment. If you purchased a product from the Home Shopping Network, the order would also be entered into a computer and stored as a backup. The only difference is that the credit-card number is traveling the Internet as packets that someone may tap into. The chances of someone grabbing a credit-card number by tapping into the packet pool are even less likely than a person making a duplicate of a credit-card receipt when you make a purchase. Of course, it is possible. Everyone who uses credit cards accepts some level of risk. Legally, if someone fraudulently uses a credit card, the credit-card owner is liable for only $50.

You might be surprised how many people are willing to send their credit-card numbers via e-mail. According to Andrew Currie, president of Cyberspace Development, a server service that runs an electronic mall and storefronts, only 10 percent of customers have been reluctant to send their credit-card numbers through e-mail.

The real problem with using e-mail for credit-card transactions is verification of the person's identity. New e-mail standards should address this problem in the near future. One solution is to place credit-card numbers on file. Establishing a preregistration system lets customers safely use e-mail without using credit-card numbers for each order. The customer fills out a fax form and returns it to your business. The form can be available via e-mail or an FTP site, or it can be included in a traditional catalog or newsletter. Once customers register their credit-card information with your business, they can order products or services by sending an e-mail message. The credit-card number on file is billed, and the product is shipped to the address on file. A signature should be on file for all changes. If the account information changes, the customer can fax the change. Your business can acknowledge an order by e-mail and alert the customer to the status of the order.

The ability to create virtual businesses and take orders via e-mail depends on your bank's credit-card merchant authorization policy. Some banks will not process credit-card transactions that arrive via e-mail. If your business is already accepting credit cards through a storefront, most likely there will be no problem with doing virtual business. However, if you are trying to establish a business to be conducted exclusively in cyberspace, getting the capability to accept credit cards is difficult. This is because credit-card merchant accounts for virtual businesses fall within the mail-order category, and most banks consider mail-order operations a high risk.

Several important initiatives are making it possible to perform secure transactions via e-mail. The CommerceNet organization has developed a special encryption system that includes a secure method for working with digital signatures and financial transactions over the Internet, particularly for credit-card purchases.

Converting E-mail to Faxes

One of the major business tools in use today is the fax machine. You can also send faxes across the Internet by using a fax service provider. Fax service providers direct the e-mail message to a fax machine, and sometimes a fax message to an e-mail address. To send a fax, you first need to set up an account with the fax provider. When you need to send a fax, you send an e-mail message to the fax provider, which in turn sends a fax.

One of the first national commercial providers is AnyWare Associates in Boston, which offers FAXiNET. The fax service receives e-mail messages from hundreds of Internet users worldwide and relays them to recipients via fax. Companies can save time by having employees send faxes from their terminals, rather than going through the usual time-consuming fax routine of preparing a cover sheet and transmitting through a fax machine. One drawback is that the Internet may not be as reliable as services offered by Sprint or MCI. But overall, the Internet appears to provide reliable service for business use.

Because Internet transmission charges are less than long-distance phone charges normally used for faxes, this e-mail fax system is a cheap way to send faxes across the country or around the world. The service is particularly popular with overseas clients who want to reach U.S. businesses, customers, and colleagues. There's an obvious cost savings, particularly for sending faxes from countries where phone rates are high. FAXiNET claims savings of up to 75 percent on telephone costs when sending a fax overseas. The service is currently available in various parts of the world, including some locations in Europe, all of Japan and Australia, the Netherlands, and Ireland, as well as sites in the United States.

To use the system, e-mail users include a fax telephone number in the address portion of their message. The mail, which may include text and graphics, is then automatically routed to a site that has agreed to serve as a local geographic cell for delivery of the fax message. The fax cell sites are computers on the Internet that are also connected to inexpensive computer-controlled fax modems that can route the files to virtually any fax machine. The cells are established cooperatively by Internet users who agree to route incoming messages to their fax destinations.

❑ ESTABLISHING AN E-MAIL SERVER PRESENCE

You can create a mailbot server that automatically bounces back a single message to users who request information, or you can create a more sophisticated mailing-list server that sends out any information you want, when you want, to Internet users who subscribe to it. The following sections explain options for establishing both types of e-mail servers.

Setting Up a Mailbot Server

Setting up a mailbot is an effective way to deliver information on demand. Once you set it up, it operates automatically. When the mail server receives an e-mail message from an Internet user, it takes the information from the From field or the message body and sends a standard response. You can change the message it sends at any time. Setting up multiple mailbots lets your business deliver several documents via e-mail. Some common uses of mailbots are as follows:

- Answers to frequently asked questions, such as your company's mailing address, business hours, and advertising information

- Company profile and product history that lists your company's background and products

- Directory of departments and who to contact, with phone numbers and e-mail addresses

- Press releases for new products and services

- Product history that includes a comparative analysis or reviews of your products and services

- Product information, such as where to buy the product, product specifications, and warranty information

- Product support that includes notes and information on accessory products

Some service providers let you establish a mailbot server on their computer or offer options for creating a mail server. HoloNet, for example, offers a simple mailing-list manager known as HoloMailer. HoloNet charges a one-time setup fee for HoloMailer service that includes a domain name for $125. Usage is billed a 5 cents per message plus $1 per megabyte of mail sent. You need to select a service name for your mailer service. This name is used as part of the mailing address that is used to get a file. For example, when you send mail to address *catalog@mailer.bookware.com*, you receive the file catalog.

To establish a mailbot on a service provider's computer, you need to use a UNIX filter program. These programs let you filter messages and automatically respond with an e-mail message, depending on the address. As with most UNIX programs, be prepared to spend some time setting a filter up. The most popular and versatile UNIX mail-filter program is Procmail. It is fast and includes several error-checking features. The Deliver mail-filter program lets you write scripts, which are miniprograms, to perform actions on incoming mail. If you're using the elm mail program, check out a program named Filter. Mailagent is another mail-filter program that lets you write scripts. Be aware that creating a mail address and filter is only the first step. You still need to publicize the mail address so that people can request the information. Figure 5.6 shows a sample of a mail-filter program to automatically respond to incoming e-mail.

FIGURE 5.6

A mail-filter program lets you automatically respond to an incoming message

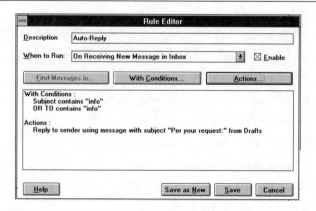

Setting Up a Mailing-List Server

A mailing-list server offers the most flexibility for sending information to people on an ongoing basis. Setting up a mailing-list server lets people subscribe to your service to receive anything you specify. Mailing lists give your business the option of having an interactive forum for your customers, so you can receive and reply to customer's comments. There are two types of mailing lists: unmoderated and moderated (or peered). In unmoderated mailing lists, messages sent to the mailing list are automatically sent to all people on the list. In a moderated mailing list, contributors send their messages to the list moderator, who chooses which messages to retransmit to the list. A moderated mailing list is really the only choice for a business-related mailing list.

Some service providers, such as Netcom, allow registered users to install and run mail servers free of charge, but users must install and maintain the server themselves. You use a mailing-list program to create a mailing-list server at your service provider's site, or you can use a server service. Setting up a mailing-list server on a service provider's computer is complex and demanding. Instead, you may want to use a server service to set up a mailing list.

Most server services will set up and maintain mailing-list services. For example, a service can set up a system to automatically mail out your newsletter or other document on a regular basis via e-mail to anyone with an e-mail address. Cyberspace Development adds a unique twist to using e-mail servers with its electronic store fronts. Mail can be sent to the storefront server, and the latest files are sent in response. This e-mail interface makes Gopher and World-Wide Web storefronts accessible to even more people, since e-mail can be handled by any online service with an e-mail gateway to the Internet—which is almost every service.

Understanding E-mail List Service Programs

The best known e-mailing list program is LISTSERV, which stands for list service. The term LISTSERV is also used generically for all mailing-list programs. In general, all these programs work in a similar manner. LISTSERV works like this. Each group has an e-mail address. The person begins by subscribing to your list. The e-mail address then acts like a mail reflector. Every time someone sends a message to the LISTSERV group, everyone who has subscribed to the list gets a copy of the mail. And every time you send a message to a group, everyone else on the list gets a copy. A LISTSERV group is usually moderated to manage what gets sent out. People voluntarily subscribe and unsubscribe to your LISTSERV group by sending an e-mail message.

Several mailing-list programs are available. The most popular is Majordomo, written by Brent Chapman. Some of the more popular UNIX mailing-list manager (MLM) software includes LISTSERV (not the same as the BITNET program of the same name), TULP (The UNIX LISTSERV Program), and the Majordomo server. Less popular mail-server programs include Squirrel Mail Server and Almanac Mail Server. Be aware that different service providers have different rules for working with mailing-list programs, and that no two mailing-list programs work the same way.

Taking a Look at a Mailing List in Action

After seven years of broadcasting on KQED, a public broadcasting station in the San Francisco Bay Area, Sedge Thomson and Michael Faklis left in 1993 to start the radio show "West Coast Live." Mike used to put newsletters together, and he found that it was a time-consuming task and was getting rather expensive. His audience was growing, and he realized he needed a new way to handle future growth. Rather than have his audience wait for a semiannual newsletter, he put together his own mailing list. As the radio station received the mail, Mike parsed the e-mail addresses and sent the first mailing out as a group alias. This proved a little cumbersome, since every time someone wanted to get added or deleted, Mike had to manually delete the name from the mail alias. Using the elm mail program, he also ran into limits that were set by his service provider. The service provider allowed the alias to contain only 75 names. Mike created several group aliases, but keeping the mailing list with all the aliases was difficult.

Mike was inspired by a newsletter created by the moderator of the rec.radio.broadcasting newsgroup that summarized the postings in the newsgroup. Mike set up a subscription mailing list. At first, Mike wanted to set up a network news (USENET) group, but he realized that a lot of people don't use network news and many people use e-mail at work. He then thought of using a mail program that used the MIME protocol so he could send sound files, but he found the limitations were too great. "You can't use MIME if you want to address the general public. The files could not be handled by all the e-mail gateways, and MIME e-mail sound files tended to be large," he said. He found that some users had restrictions; for example, at least one user used radio mail, so he could read only the first 400 lines of a message, and graphic and sound files were out of the question. Mike decided to use e-mail to distribute his newsletter and had Netcom set up a LISTSERV at no cost. Mike also uses filters for promotions; for example, when he sends out the newsletter, he announces the number of the broadcast, so on the 25th show, the 25th person sending e-mail to the address *westcoastlive.netcom.com* that contains the phrase *free ticket drawing* receives two free tickets to the show. To subscribe to the mailing list, send an e-mail message that looks like this:

To: listserv@netcom.com
Subject: <leave blank>
Skip down to the body of the message and type:
subscribe westcoastlive *your name*

❑ PROMOTING YOUR E-MAIL PRESENCE

Promote your e-mail addresses in all your business documents. Consider your e-mail address as important as you would a telephone or fax number. For example, if you mail out a newsletter, include your e-mail addresses where appropriate. Another way to use your e-mail address to advertise your business presence is to add it to your stationery and business cards. Include e-mail addresses in any advertising, such as display ads. Promoting your e-mail address is in your business interest from both a customer-service perspective and a business-cost perspective.

You should publicize your mailing list and any mailbot addresses you have in any advertising media you already use, such as your company newsletter or press releases. You can try a few lists of mailing lists to see if you can add to your mailing list. The most popular is a file named MAIL-LIST.TXT, which is maintained by Stephanie de Silva (*arielle@taronga.com*).

Chapter 6

□ □ □

Tapping into Network News for Research and Promotion

Network news, also known as USENET news, is a distributed messaging system with an estimated 10 million participants. Thousands of ongoing network news discussions cover every topic imaginable. People who subscribe to network news communicate using a messaging system that is similar to e-mail. Businesses can use network news to participate in forums in areas of shared interests as well as to conduct communication with potential customers. This chapter explains using network news for commercial activities, including how network news works and the rules governing the individual newsgroups.

□ HOW NETWORK NEWS WORKS

Network news is delivered via the UNIX-based network known as USENET. USENET is not actually part of the Internet, but it is widely available because so many systems on the Internet are running UNIX. Today even non-UNIX computers can participate in USENET news. Each USENET site collects and sends information to other sites. These sites, in turn, add their items and then forward them. In this way, articles are propagated throughout the network. As of January 1993, more than 700,000 sites were receiving network news, and over 10 million people were participating. USENET discussions are called *newsgroups*. Each newsgroup refers to a particular topic and contains *articles* (messages) related to that topic that are *posted* (sent) by individuals. Network news includes special newsgroups that include binary files, which can be downloaded.

The Structure of Network Newsgroups

Newsgroups are dynamic: They are continually being created or elimi-nated. The groups are structured hierarchically, with the main topic appear-ing first, followed by subtopics. The name of each topic and its subtopics are separated by periods. For example, the newsgroup biz.misc is a news-group concentrating on miscellaneous commercial business topics. Newsgroups are either moderated or unmoderated. A moderated news-group is a discussion group where a moderator decides whether to post a submission, weighing its relevance to the forum. An unmoderated news-group has no one filtering postings. The following list describes the main newsgroup topics defined in network news.

Newsgroup Topic	Description
alt	Alternative newsgroups that vary in subject matter, ranging from political activism to sex stories
biz	Business-related topics
comp	Computer science and related topics, including software sources and information on hardware and software systems
misc	Topics that don't fit into other categories or that fit into several categories
news	Information on network news and USENET
rec	Hobbies, recreational activities, and the arts
sci	Scientific research and applications of computer science
soc	Social issues, where *social* can mean politically relevant to socializing, or anything in between
talk	A forum for debate on controversial topics

Many newsgroups are targeted at a particular region and distributed only within that region. These newsgroups are identified by a multiple-letter code. Table 6.1 lists these regional newsgroups for the United States.

TABLE 6.1
Geographical Distributions on USENET

Geographical Area	Newsgroup
Akron, OH	akron
Ann Arbor, MI	aa
Arizona	az
Atlanta, GA	atl
Austin, TX	austin
California	ca
Chicago, IL	chi
Chico, CA	chico
Cleveland, OH	cle
Colorado	co
Columbus, OH	cmh
Dallas-Ft. Worth, TX	dfw
Des Moines, IA	dsm
Detroit, MI	det
Florida	fl
Georgia	ga
Houston, TX	houston
Huntsville, AL	hsv
Illinois	il
Indiana	in
Iowa	ia
Iowa City, IA	iowacity
Kansas	ks
Kansas City, KS	kc
Kentucky	ky
Los Angeles, CA	la
Louisiana	lou
Manhattan, KS	mhk
Maryland	md
Melbourne, FL	mlb
Miami, FL	miami
Michigan	mi
Milwaukee, WI	milw

(continued on next page)

TABLE 6.1 (continued)

Geographical Area	Newsgroup
Minnesota	mn
Missouri	mo
New England (CT, MA, ME, NH, RI, VT)	ne
New Jersey	nj
New Orleans, LA	neworleans
New York City	ny
North Carolina	nc
Ohio	oh
Oklahoma	ok
Orange County, CA	oc
Oregon	or
Orlando, FL	oau
Pacific Northwest (ID, OR, WA)	pnw
Pennsylvania	pa
Philadelphia, PA	phl
Pittsburgh, PA	pgh
Portland, OR	pdx
Research Triangle Park Area, NC	triangle
Rio Grande Valley, NM	rg
Sacramento, CA	sac
San Diego County, CA	sdnet
San Francisco Bay Area, CA	ba
Santa Barbara, CA	sba
Santa Clara and Santa Cruz counties, CA	sbay
Santa Cruz County, CA	scruz
Sarasota, FL	sarasota
Seattle, WA	seattle
Seattle, WA	sea
South Bay region (San Francisco Bay Area), CA	sbay
St. Louis, MO	stl
Tampa Bay area, FL	tba
Tennessee	tn
Texas	tx

Geographical Area	Newsgroup
Tidewater, VA	tdw
Utah	utah
Virginia	va
Washington	wa
Washington, DC	dc
Western N.Y. (Rochester, Buffalo)	wny
Wisconsin	wi

A Day in the Life of a Network News User

To work with network news, Internet users need an account with a service provider and a client newsreader program. There are many ways to read network news, and many newsreader programs are available. Newsreader programs let users control which newsgroups they want to subscribe to, read articles, save articles to files, respond to articles, post articles, and transfer files. Because thousands of newsgroups are available, newsreaders are important tools for managing the number of newsgroups a user participates in.

Internet users who are not using an IP account usually use a UNIX-based newsreader program. UNIX newsreaders include tin, nn, trn, and rn. These newsreader programs are more difficult to use than the GUI-based rewsreaders used by IP account users. Additionally, using newsreaders to post messages is difficult because they usually use the UNIX program's vi editor—an unfriendly text editor. Figure 6.1 shows a newsgroup listing as it appears from a non-IP account user, Figure 6.2, a newsgroup article.

For IP account connections, a growing number of Windows, Macintosh, and X Windows (UNIX) newsreader programs are available. These TCP/IP newsreaders use the Network News Transfer Protocol (NNTP) to transfer news. It's easier to work with network news using TCP/IP newsreader programs, although it may be slower than using a UNIX-based reader on a service provider's computer. This is because the newsgroups are fed to your local computer instead of being read from the service provider's computer. A big advantage of using a TCP/IP newsreader is that it's easier to manage and post network news articles using these programs. Figure 6.3 shows a newsgroup listing, and Figure 6.4 shows an article in the Trumpet newsreader program. See the appendix for a listing of TCP/IP newsreader programs.

FIGURE 6.1

How a newsgroup listing appears to a non-IP account user

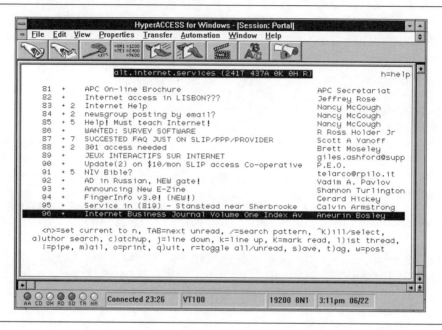

FIGURE 6.2

How a newsgroup article appears to a non-IP account user

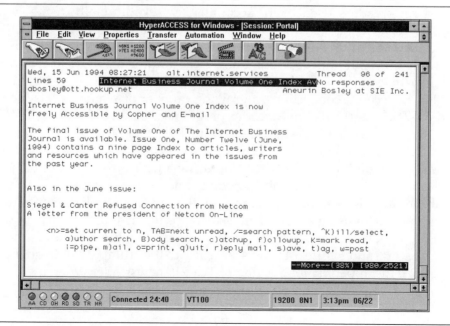

FIGURE 6.3

A newsgroup listing appearing in the Trumpet newsreader

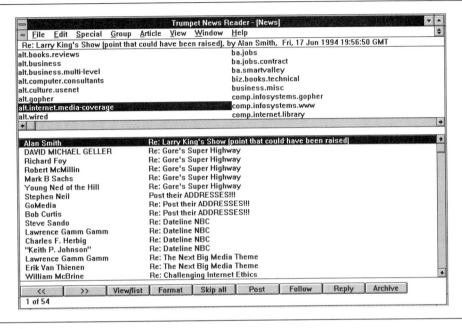

FIGURE 6.4

A newsgroup article appearing in the Trumpet newsreader

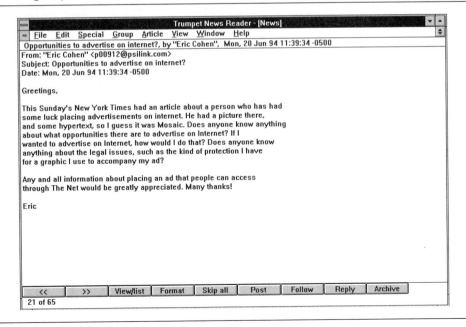

❏ MANAGING NETWORK NEWSGROUPS FOR YOUR COMPANY

Your business may want to have employees participate in business-related newsgroups, but people tend to spend a lot of time having fun with network news. Because one of the fundamental principles of network news is the absence of censorship, a lot of distractions are available, such as humor and erotica newsgroups. Giving everyone access to network news may not be in the best interests of your business. Network news is fed to your local computer system as part of your IP account. You must control access to network news at your local site.

❏ USING NETWORK NEWS TO PROMOTE YOUR BUSINESS

In general, the USENET community is a hostile environment for businesses, and many newsgroups are hanging out a No Soliciting sign. If you have a product or service that matches a newsgroup and you have the time to be an active participant in the forum, then you can build credibility, successfully promote your goods and services, and be seen as a responsible part of the Internet business community. Posting articles in several newsgroups is called *cross-posting*. Cross-posting articles to relevant newsgroups is acceptable, but cross-posting and deliberately disregarding the interests of specific newsgroups is known as *spamming*. Posting advertisements in any newsgroup or spamming can result in extensive damage to your business. Network news users have ways to overwhelm your business, such as flooding you with angry e-mail messages, posting articles attached to your article or ad that publicly criticize your business, and more.

A Case of Network News Abuse

In April 1994, a husband-and-wife law firm named Canter & Siegel, based in Phoenix, posted an unsolicited advertisement to over 5,000 newsgroups. The ad solicited foreign nationals willing to pay $95 per person for help in filling out the forms necessary to participate in a U.S. government lottery. A total of 55,000 winners of this lottery would in turn be awarded green-card work permits, which extend permanent residency status to immigrants. In return, the lawyers received 30,000 angry e-mail messages. The flames (angry e-mail) even included death threats. The mail-bombing programs set

100

up by angry network news users repeatedly crashed Internet Direct's system (Canter & Siegel's service provider). Internet Direct suspended Canter & Siegel's account for violating the customer service agreement. The lawyers threatened to sue for $250,000 to recover the messages from people interested in their offer. Individuals jammed the law firm's telephone, fax machine, and computer systems for days afterward. This is not to say that posting can't be profitable; Canter & Siegel said they made money from their post, and they plan to do it again. The bottom line is that this type of approach to using network news is bad business.

The Future of Commercial Use of Network News

A plan was recently announced by the Internet Company to create acceptable advertising zones on USENET where companies could place commercial advertising, product information, promotional offers, and price lists. Two other companies are offering to create advertising zones on USENET news. These advertising zones would require advertisers to pay a fee to place their messages on the network.

Posting Guidelines

How easy or difficult it is to post a news article depends on the newsreader program you are using. Many non-IP (UNIX-based) account newsreaders default to the vi editor, which is difficult to use. If you're using a UNIX-based newsreader, such as tin, change to the pine editor to make it easier to post articles. Using an IP account newsreader to post an article is typically as easy as sending a mail message. Figure 6.5 shows an article being posted in the Trumpet newsreader.

Before you create your article, you need to understand some basic guidelines. The following are several general guidelines for posting to newsgroups.

- Post announcements of professional products or services that will be of overall benefit to the readers on that newsgroup. Don't post to a general-purpose newsgroup. Clearly mark your article as a product announcement in the subject line. Don't repeat a product announcement. Inappropriate announcements or articles violating this policy are usually rejected.

- Post local articles only to the geographical areas that will be interested. Few people outside you local area will care if your product is only of local interest. See if there is an appropriate geographically

FIGURE 6.5

Posting a newsgroup article using the Trumpet newsreader

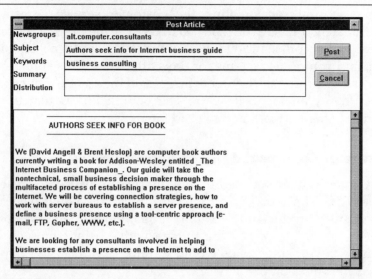

limited newsgroup in which to post your article (see Table 6.1 for a listing of local newsgroups). These local newsgroups offer a more focused market for businesses operating in their respective region.

- Keep cross-posting to a minimum.

- Don't post messages in newsgroups reserved for files or for a specific purpose. For example, *news.newusers.questions* is intended for queries, *alt.binaries.pictures* is only for graphics files, *rec.humor* is only for posting jokes, and *misc.wanted* is for want ads. Discussions for newsgroups designated for files belong in a similarly named newsgroup that ends with the extension *.d*.

- Don't post the same article more than once in the same newsgroup. The default expiration for a posted article is normally in the range of 7 to 21 days.

- Test posting an article by posting a message to the local *misc.test* newsgroup (which is used for that purpose) before posting your article to a specific newsgroup.

- Take time to browse the newsgroup to which you intend to post a message. Read what other people post, and notice the group's reaction to commercial messages. If a press release or product announcement is met with intense flaming, then do not risk alienating this group of Internet users with your commercial message.

- Read any articles posted to a newsgroup named FAQ (frequently asked questions). You can find helpful FAQs for using USENET news in the newsgroups *news.answers*, *news.newusers.questions*, and *news.announce.newusers*. Read any newsgroup's FAQ file, if it has one, before you post an article. This file explains what the nature of the newsgroup is and what is acceptable for the newsgroup.

Creating an Effective Article

Network news is not a mass market, but a constellation of microforums, each with its own distinct history, rules, and concerns. The challenge of promoting your business using network news is creating the right type of article and posting it to the correct newsgroup. Writing an article to post is similar to writing an e-mail message, with additional conventions. Here are some guidelines to keep in mind as you create an article for posting to a newsgroup.

- Make your article short and to the point. Many people on the Internet are busy. Direct the readers to another source for additional information. It's important to realize that the Internet is being read by many different types of computers.

- Don't use special characters or control characters in an article. That way, everyone can read your message without problems. In fact, the space character is about the only one you can be sure will work consistently. Make your article fit in the first two screens (about 50 lines) in length, and keep your article lines under 80 characters in width—under 72 lines, if possible.

- Don't use traditional advertising copy with style, image, and hype. It will not go over well on network news. Stick to facts. Readers of network news appreciate quality, filtered information, so find a way to add value to your message. Couch your article within a commentary. Express your own opinions.

- Include only short extracts of a copyrighted work for critical purposes. Reproduction in whole is strictly and explicitly forbidden by U.S. and international copyright law.

- Be careful when you refer to other articles. Refer to articles by message ID, not by article number. The position of articles varies from system to system.

- Don't use excerpts from private e-mail correspondence in your article without the permission of the author of the article. Under copyright statutes, the author of the e-mail message possesses a copyright on mail that he or she wrote.

- Don't forget that anyone can read your article, including your competitors.

- Include a signature in your article, as explained in the following section.

Use a Signature in Your Articles

Network news users often append information to the end of their messages. The appended material is known as the signature, and it is kept within a file known as a signature file. A signature file is a text file that contains additional information about you. Information such as your e-mail address, U.S. mail address, telephone, and fax number is sufficient. If you have something particularly witty to say, you can append a one-line phrase, but anything more is likely to engender complaints. Since signatures are appended to most messages, they comprise a significant fraction of total traffic volume. To help control the volume of network traffic, users are expected to keep signatures to a minimum size. You create signature files using a text editor, and some newsreaders let you create them directly from the newsreader program. The following is a sample signature.

```
=========================================================
David Angell              |
dangell@bookware.com      |            Bookware
Vox: (415) 967-0559       |       Technical Communications
Fax: (415) 967-8283       |
For more information send e-mail to info@bookware.com
=========================================================
```

Creating a USENET Newsgroup

Rules have been devised for creating groups within the USENET newsgroup hierarchy. For example, ZEOS, the computer manufacturer, has a newsgroup called *biz.zeos.general.* By creating a forum, moderating the submissions (filtering out irrelevant postings), and providing high-quality information about your products and services, you can establish a growing readership in the same way a newspaper or newsletter does. Unfortunately, to create a newsgroup for total network distribution, the process is too complex and time-consuming for most businesses. The steps for creating a newsgroup for total distribution are as follows:

1. Request for discussion (RFD). Post an RFD to *news.announce.newgroups* and in groups or mailing lists relevant to the topic. All the details of the conference need not be worked out prior to the RFD announcement, since this is one of the reasons for the discussion period. Actual discussion of the RFD takes place in newsgroups. The goal of the discussion period is to come to agreement on aspects of the proposal, such as whether the group is needed at all, and if so, whether it should be moderated (and who will moderate) and what the group should be called.

2. Call for votes (CFV). After discussion has crystallized and it is decided that the group is needed, a CFV announcement is issued in *news.announce.newgroups.* The CFV announcement should include instructions on how to vote. A fair chance must be given to yes or no proponents; often, this is done by establishing mail servers for yes and no proponents, both on the same machine. CFV announcements are repeated during the voting period to remind people of the ongoing vote.

3. Voting. Voting periods last 21 to 30 days, after which time votes are tallied and a list of voters and how they voted is posted to *news.announce.newgroups* for verification. Winning groups must have at least 100 more yes than no votes and at least a 66 percent favorable response. Groups that are voted down must wait at least six months to be voted on again. During the process, the moderator of *news.announce.newgroups* will post a periodic message on the status of the various proposals, as well as listings of newly created groups. The results of votes are also posted to this group.

Creating an alt (alternative) group is considerably simpler, which is why many new groups are begun in this hierarchy. This is not always a wise decision, since alt groups are distributed less widely than core USENET groups. If it is intended that a group eventually become a core USENET group, it may make more sense to start the group there. Once a group has been started in the alt hierarchy, it may not be easy to get people to switch to the equivalent core group if it is created.

Chapter 7

Sharing Your Business Information with FTP

FTP is a popular vehicle for sharing information and software across the Internet. Almost everyone connected to the Internet has access to FTP to quickly transfer files. For businesses, FTP offers affordable opportunities for setting up an FTP server to share information in file form, or to distribute software to all Internet users or to a select group of people. This chapter explains how your business can use FTP to share files.

❑ WHAT IS FTP, AND HOW DOES IT WORK?

FTP stands for File Transfer Protocol. This protocol lets client programs transfer files to and from FTP servers. IP account Internet users have several FTP client program options available. The FTP program is standard fare on most PC and Macintosh TCP/IP client packages. It's also built into most versions of the UNIX operating system, which is used by most shell- and menu-account Internet users. FTP sites can also be accessed using Gopher and the World-Wide Web.

Public FTP file archives are called *anonymous FTP* sites. The term *anonymous* refers to a generic account that can be used by anyone to log into an FTP server. Thousands of anonymous sites are scattered throughout the Internet. Many of these file archives let users get programs and other files at no charge. Most anonymous FTP servers restrict users to a single directory for uploading files, and some don't let users upload files at all for security reasons. Private FTP servers allow sensitive files to be transferred among a select group of people. Whether files can be downloaded and uploaded depends on how an FTP server is set up.

A Day in the Life of an FTP User

FTP users connect to an FTP server and log in with their user name and password. If they're connecting to an anonymous FTP server, they enter *anonymous* as their user name, then enter their e-mail address or guest. Once users are connected to the FTP server, they navigate the server's file system. Figure 7.1 shows a typical directory and file listing on an FTP server from a non-IP account user's perspective. Figures 7.2 and 7.3 show a typical directory and file listing using graphical FTP client programs available to IP users (Windows and Macintosh programs). Users change directories to get to the directory they want, then display a list of the contents of a directory.

FTP servers typically include text files that provide information about the files located at that FTP server. Text files can be read online by most FTP client programs. The README file, found at most FTP sites, contains information about the site or the files within a directory. Directories that include a large number of files sometimes offer an INDEX file that contains information about the files in the directory. Some sites include the file ls-lR, which

FIGURE 7.1

How an FTP site looks to a non-IP account user

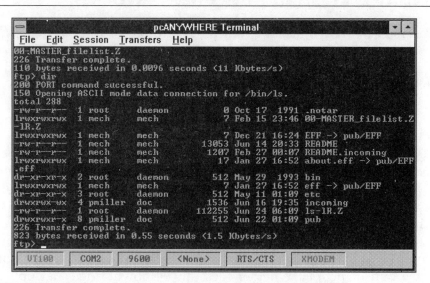

FIGURE 7.2

How an FTP site looks to an IP user using Chameleon on a PC

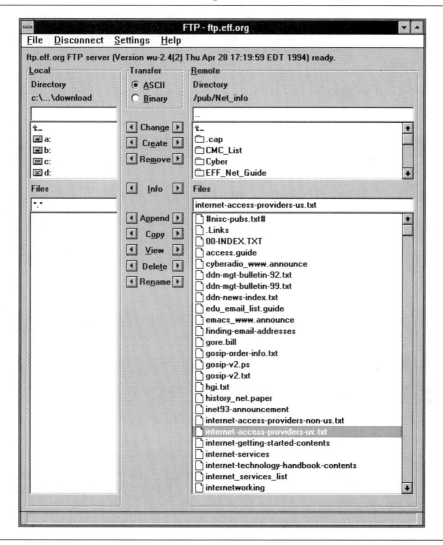

FIGURE 7.3

How an FTP site looks to an IP user using Fetch on a Macintosh

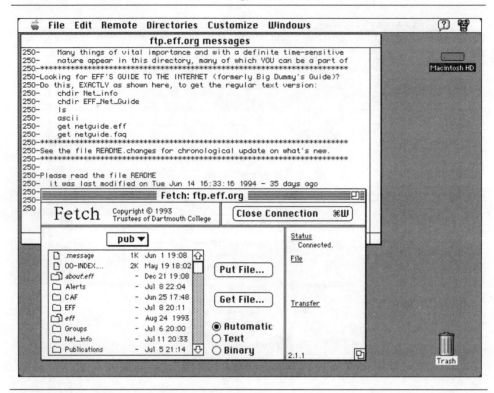

includes a comprehensive listing of all directories and the files included in them that are available on the FTP server.

FTP users work with two main categories of file types: ASCII and binary. An ASCII file is a text file—the most universal format because it can be read on any computer system, even online. Binary files are encoded with control characters and include programs and files that can be used by specific programs. Text files that are compressed are classified as binary. Beyond these two broad categories, FTP users must identify the file as being able to work on their system. Because the Internet is a melting pot for all kinds of computer systems and file types, many FTP sites organize files according to computing platforms.

Files are compressed to save storage space and reduce the time it takes to transfer files. Because most files stored at FTP sites are compressed, FTP users need to be able to recognize a file that is compressed and the program that was used to compact the file. Several techniques for data compression exist, and consequently several different compression programs are used. Once you download a compressed file, you must uncompress it. Compressed files are usually flagged by the suffix or extension on the file name.

File-naming conventions help FTP users identify different file types, their compression status, and the compression utility used. For example, a file with the extension .ZIP is a PC (DOS/Windows) file that has been compressed with the compression program PKZIP. A file that ends with .SIT is a Macintosh file that has been compressed with the StuffIt compression program.

Once FTP users find the files they want, they can download a single file or multiple files to their client computer. Users accessing the Internet through a non-IP account transfer files to the service provider's computer from the FTP server, not directly to their own computer. Non-IP account users must perform the additional step of downloading the files from the service provider's computer to their computer. Likewise, files are first uploaded to the service provider's computer and then to the FTP host computer. Users accessing the Internet via IP accounts can transfer files directly between their computer and the FTP server.

❏ DESIGNING YOUR FTP SERVER

Your business can set up either an anonymous FTP site to deliver information to any Internet user or a secured FTP server to handle sensitive files. Establishing an FTP presence involves designing the directory structure you want, then setting up the FTP server. An FTP site helps solve the problem of distributing files for multiple platforms. Different mail programs have different limitations, and if you need to transfer binary files to different platforms, it is safer to use an FTP site so other people can download the files directly. For example, by letting others know of your FTP site, you can store and share executable programs for different platforms.

An anonymous FTP site is a cost-effective way to deliver information to Internet users. Many service providers let you set up a directory in their anonymous FTP directory for other users to access the files. Private FTP sites cannot typically be set up at a service provider, and depending on the amount of traffic, you may need to set up a private FTP site using a server service.

Regardless of the type of FTP site you want to establish, you need to design your FTP site. For example, you need to know what files you want to make available, how you want to organize the files for different platforms, how to compress files, and so on. For example, a bookstore selling books to Mac users might include its newsletter, catalog, price lists, order forms, and possibly a HyperCard order form. These files can include information on how customers can contact the bookstore, such as e-mail, an 800 phone number, fax, or snail mail. Customers can in turn download these files to read and run at their local site. The following sections explain the key issues you need to understand before setting up your FTP site.

Determining the Files You Want to Make Available

You should always include files in ASCII text format. In addition, you can also make files available in different formats for different platforms. If you are going to have files in formats for different platforms, you need to decide what formats you're going to make available. For example, many FTP sites contain PostScript files for UNIX and Macintosh users. Creating files in different formats for different programs can be time-consuming. Do not create files for different platforms by simply exporting them from an application on a different platform. The export features of most programs are not foolproof, and chances are that not all the formatting will be changed correctly. Here are some of the popular formats for sharing files with different platforms:

- ASCII text is standard text that can be displayed on any computer. ASCII text files usually end with the file-name extension .txt.

- PostScript files can be printed on any PostScript printer. Some programs, such as GhostScript, let you view PostScript files. PostScript files are transferred as ASCII files because they don't include control characters. PostScript files usually end in the file-name extension .ps.

- Rich text format (RTF) is text that includes formatting, such as bold, italic, and underlined text. It cannot contain any graphic images. RTF files typically end with the file-name extension .rtf.

- Portable document format (PDF) files can be read using Adobe Acrobat Reader. The Reader for version 2.0 is available free for the three main platforms: UNIX, PC (DOS/Windows), and Macintosh. Virtually any document can be converted into a PDF file. PDF documents can also include hypertext links to link multiple documents. With version 2.0, Adobe has opened the PDF architecture to developers, so links can be made with existing Internet programs, such as Gopher and Mosaic. PDF documents can also be secured to prevent unwanted copying, pasting, or printing. PDF files end with the filename extension .PDF.

- Common Ground files can be stored and read on different platforms. The document file is stored with a built-in veiwer. When a person opens a Common Ground document, the viewer program automatically loads the document. Common Ground makes files available for the PC (DOS/Windows) and Macintosh platforms. Common Ground files can be secured to prevent unwanted copying, pasting, and printing and are usually stored as executable files. Common Ground documents end with a .dp extension for the Macintosh and an .exe extension for Windows.

- Macintosh DiskPaper file format converts Macintosh documents into stand-alone applications that can be viewed or printed, pixel for pixel, with the same quality as the original documents. This format is especially useful for distributing documents created by graphic or presentation software, such as PowerPoint.

- HyperCard is a Macintosh hypertext and database program, and its files are usually referred to as HyperCard stacks. These stacks are usually stored in a compressed format, typically using the StuffIt compression program (StuffIt files end with the extension .sit).

- HTML stands for HyperText Markup Language, which is used to create World-Wide Web documents that can be viewed by Mosaic or other Web browsers. Because HTML files are text files, they can be read using the X Windows, Microsoft Windows, or Macintosh versions of Mosaic or other Web browsers. See Chapter 9 for more information on the World-Wide Web, Mosaic, and HTML.

Sharing Software and Copyright Restrictions

If you decide to include any software programs, you should be aware of the type of restrictions that apply to distributing the software. Software falls into four main categories:

- Public-domain software is not copyrighted. The author has created the software to be freely shared with no limitations. Even the code of public-domain software can be changed.

- Freeware is software where the author has retained the copyright. You can give freeware away, but you cannot alter the code.

- Shareware is based on the premise that if you try it and want to continue to use the software, you pay the author a minimal fee after an evaluation period. The author retains the copyright. You can freely distribute shareware, but without express permission of the author, you cannot charge for it. Shareware is a better alternative than public-domain software or freeware for most businesses because you can get technical support if you are in a jam.

- Commercial software is copyrighted and sold as is for profit. Distributing commercial software without permission is a criminal offense.

Some FTP sites work with companies to make software updates available. For example, the Oakland University (*oak.oakland.edu*) offers updates that you can use to update existing copies of commercial programs such as AfterDark, FileMaker Pro, ProComm, or CrossTalk.

Compressing Large Files

Disks have a nasty habit of filling up, and FTP directories are no exception. Compressing files can save between 40 and 60 percent of the file space. Not all files benefit from compression; for example, some graphics files, such as GIF and JPG, don't need to be compressed. Despite the added inconvenience of decompressing the file, most users appreciate compressed files because it means files can be transferred in less time.

The type of compression used should be consistent, as well as appropriate to the files being compressed. The compression should match the platform for which the file is intended, not the platform on which the FTP server is running. Certain compression programs are becoming standard for different platforms. PKZIP is used by most PC (DOS and Windows) users, StuffIt files are used by most Mac users, and compress, tar, and GNU zip are the standard compression programs used for UNIX files.

Even if files are stored in ASCII format, for large files you may want to use a compression program. Be sure to let your users know which compression methods you use by putting a note in the README file. A simple comment in each relevant directory can save users a lot of frustration. Such pointers are particularly important if you use a new or nontraditional type of compression.

Remember that compressed files need to be uncompressed at the client end before they are usable. Making the compression programs available on your server, if possible, will be greatly appreciated by your users. Another alternative is to include instructions for downloading the appropriate compression program from another FTP site.

Determining Your Security Needs

You can create directories that limit or grant permissions to access files. For example, you can create one directory that lets users get files only from that directory, and create another directory that lets people upload files. You may want one directory for incoming files and another directory for outgoing files. If your FTP site is going to handle incoming files, you need to make sure the directories are set up with read and write permissions. A directory for incoming files will require more system administration time, however. As many FTP administrators will attest, the downside to having an incoming directory is that someone has to continually check the directory.

If you let users upload files, the possibility of a virus attacking your network becomes a major security concern. Your first line of defense must be careful scrutiny of all uploaded files. Virus-detection programs are available that let you examine the uploaded files for any problems. Be sure to run the virus program before you run the uploaded programs or make them available to other users.

Structuring Directories to Organize Your Files

How you present your files is important so people can access the right file. Descriptive, well-organized directories make it easier for people to get the right files. Keeping files organized and up to date can be a time-consuming task. Don't set up an anonymous FTP site if you can't keep the files up to date. If the directories are empty, make sure you delete them.

Most computers use a hierarchical file structure. When users log into an FTP site, they're at the root directory. The root directory is indicated as a backslash (\) on UNIX systems and a slash (/) on PC systems. Subdirectories are listed with the slash before the directory name; for example, on a PC a subdirectory might be /pub. Each subsequent directory down in the hierarchy is listed with a slash; for example, /pub/catalog. To create an effective directory structure, make directories for storing files for the plat-forms you want to support. For example, you may have a directory structure similar to the one shown in Figure 7.4.

FIGURE 7.4
A sample directory structure

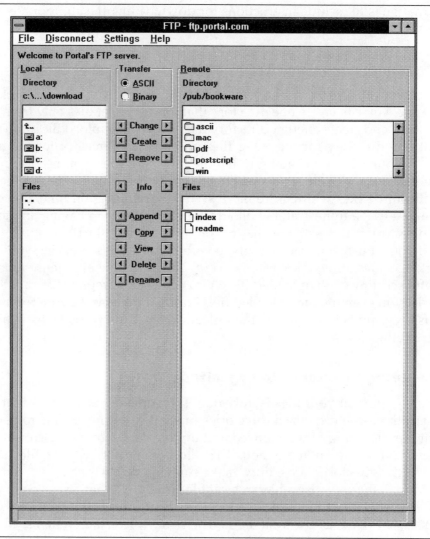

Informing Users What Files Are Available

Foremost among the things you should consider is a listing of the entire contents of your FTP server. Typically, listings for UNIX servers are files named ls-1R or FILELIST placed in the top-level directory. The ls-1R comes from the UNIX ls -r (list) command, which stands for a listing that recursively displays each directory and its contents. Directories that include a large number of files sometimes offer an INDEX file that contains information about the files in the directory. On an active server, your INDEX file should be updated weekly or biweekly; on less active servers, a monthly update may suffice. However, you should update the listing regularly so users will know when to check it.

Include an ASCII text README file in the top-level directory. The README file can contain information such as the purpose of the site and the name and e-mail address of the person maintaining it. This file should explain the directory structure and identify how you are compressing files. It can also point out other methods to retrieve the information or include instructions for getting the file compression program used to compress the files. Within each subdirectory, you can add another README or INDEX file to describe the contents. These files can include information related to the files in the directory. README files can quickly become outdated, so it's a good idea to keep their descriptions fairly generic.

Some new FTP servers let you display a message when a person enters the cd command to change to a different directory. You can inform the user what type of files are stored in the directory. Be aware that most IP graphical client programs display this information only if a log window is open. If you or your server service create a message of this type, keep it short. Long messages can confuse some client programs.

❏ SETTING UP YOUR FTP SERVER

The easiest way to establish an anonymous FTP server is to set up your FTP site on a service provider's computer system. Most service providers let people who have an Internet access account on their system set up an anonymous FTP presence for a small fee. If you want to set up a private FTP site, you must use a server service to create and maintain your site, which costs considerably more than setting up an anonymous FTP site. Another option for setting up a secured FTP site is to establish an FTP site on a computer connected to the Internet via an IP connection. The following sections explain these options.

Setting Up an Anonymous FTP Server Using a Service Provider

Many service providers will set up an FTP directory for your business on their server for the price of renting disk space. For example, Netcom and Alternet will set up anonymous FTP sites for as little as $2.50 a month. Service providers do this as a service for their customers, so you must have an account with the service provider. Setting up an FTP presence on your service provider's network is an inexpensive solution for sharing files. It ensures that others can get the files without having your computer connected to the Internet.

Establishing an FTP presence on a service provider's computer puts your directory under a directory that the service provider has designated as an anonymous FTP site.

To establish your anonymous FTP site on a service provider's computer, you must have at least a shell account. If you have an IP account, chances are you already have a shell account, which was included with the IP account. The service provider lets only the user who owns the account that the FTP site is being charged to upload files to the anonymous FTP directory. To upload the files to the FTP directory, you must use the user name and password that you use to access your Internet account. The following are some specific questions to ask your service provider when you set up an anonymous FTP account.

- What are the costs? Usually, the service provider charges a small setup charge and a monthly storage charge per megabyte of files at your FTP site.

- What is the exact path of the directory so you can upload the files? For example, you may have to change to a directory path such as */export/home/machine1/ftp/pub/bookware* to upload your files. This is a different path than Internet users use to get to your anonymous FTP directory, which might be only */pub/bookware*.

- Does the service provider periodically clean out files from its anonymous FTP sites? If so, how often are files removed?

Setting Up an FTP Server Using a Server Service

Some service providers will not set up an anonymous FTP site on their servers. If the service provider you're using to connect to the Internet doesn't allow you to establish an anonymous FTP presence, you can contact a server service. However, because it is easy to create an anonymous FTP

118

server on the service provider's side and share files via most e-mail programs, it is not common to create an anonymous FTP server with a server service.

It's more likely that you will have a server service set up a private FTP site on its server, so only a select group of Internet users can gain access to files. For example, you may want to have a private FTP server set up so you can distribute information to salespeople in the field. In most cases, you will want to have the server service create a read-only directory. Letting several people have access creates a security risk. For example, someone could upload a pirated software program. Additionally, you must constantly monitor your FTP site to manage incoming files. Typically, private FTP sites are inexpensive relative to other server options. Because of the many variables, it is difficult for server services to quote standard prices; the options you purchase can quickly drive up the price. You should ask yourself the following questions before asking a server service to set up an FTP server:

- How much disk space will you be using?

- How often will you be updating or replacing files?

- Who will be authorized to upload files?

- How many people will have access?

- How often will people be accessing the server?

- How do you want to be billed—monthly, quarterly, or yearly?

Be aware that most server services don't have published prices for setting up a private (or anonymous) FTP site. After you know what you want, you will need to get a quote from the server service. Prices can range from a few hundred dollars to several thousand dollars a year. The best advice is to shop around.

Setting Up an FTP Server on Your Computer System

Using an IP connection and a TCP/IP program like Chameleon (Windows) or TCP Connect II (Macintosh), you can create an FTP server presence on a computer system at your business site. This option is useful if you want to create a small, secured FTP site for a few users. We don't recommend it as a way to create an anonymous FTP site for the general public. First, it's a security risk. Second, if more than a few users access your FTP server, the amount of data traffic coming to your server and the demands on your computer may be overwhelming. Because TCP/IP is a packet system, more than one user can connect to your server from the Internet, even if your server is connected using a PC and a 14.4 kbps modem. Your computer system will process multiple file-transfer requests because of the TCP/IP software's packet switching. Of course, your connection must be active to allow transfers. This can be expensive if you are using a dial-up connection. You may establish that files can be transferred only at certain hours.

To establish a private FTP site using Chameleon, you first define the users that can access your FTP site. Each user is assigned a user name, a password, and a directory path. This lets you create a secured directory for each user and give each user privacy from other users. Figure 7.5 shows the window for listing users that have access to your site. Figure 7.6 shows a dialog box used to add a user to your list. As long as you're connected to the Internet, the users you've assigned a user name and password can access the files in the shared directories.

FIGURE 7.5
The Chameleon window, listing users that have access to an FTP server

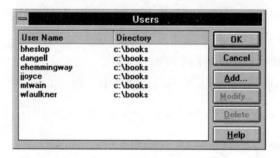

FIGURE 7.6
The Chameleon window used to add users to an FTP server

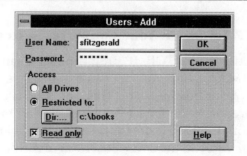

❑ HOW TO ENSURE PEOPLE CAN FIND YOUR FTP SITE

Beyond the promotional options explained in Chapter 4, you have a few other options for promoting your anonymous FTP presence. One of the most popular methods to find FTP files is by using a program named Archie. Archie is a database system that includes an extensive index of FTP sites and files. People on the Internet can either use an Archie client program or use a Telnet client program to establish a remote terminal session with an Archie server. Archie is also available from some Gopher clients and World-Wide Web browsers.

If you can't connect to Archie via Telnet, you can send mail to an Archie server with search commands in the body of the message. Archie servers survey the Internet and keep track of FTP site information. Besides keeping track of the FTP sites, the Archie server also maintains a whatis database. The whatis database cross-references numerous terms with associated file or directory names. You can search using the whatis database only by using Telnet to connect to an Archie server.

Users can find files based on parts of your file name. This is one reason to use intuitive and descriptive file names. Figure 7.7 shows the results of using an Archie client. For information on promoting your company's FTP site and files, see Chapter 4.

FIGURE 7.7
The results of using an Archie client

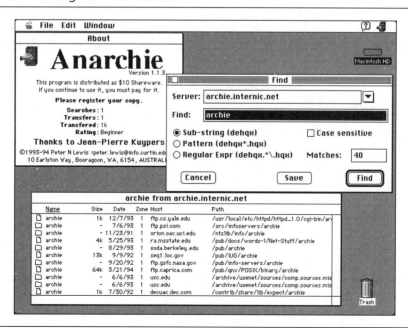

Chapter 8

❑ ❑ ❑

Establishing Your Business Presence in Gopherspace

Gopher is one of the leading workhorse tools of the Internet. It's an information system used to organize and distribute information on thousands of servers across the Internet. The thousands of Gopher sites are collectively referred to as *Gopherspace*. Gopher owes its popularity to its ease of use, its powerful search and retrieval features, and the fact that it can be accessed by any Internet user. Establishing a server presence in Gopherspace links your business to a network of Gopher servers where millions of Internet users can quickly find your site. Once at your site, they can read online text information, retrieve files, conduct business transactions, and more. This chapter explains how to set up shop and do business in Gopherspace.

❑ WHAT GOPHER IS AND HOW IT WORKS

Gopher was developed at the University of Minnesota and named after the school's mascot. It was originally designed to give on-campus Internet users easier access to internal and remote information resources. Because it is highly accessible to different sites on the Internet, Gopher quickly became a popular search and retrieval system for the Internet. It uses a simple client/server protocol that supports publishing and searching for information held on a distributed network of servers. Gopher clients have a seamless view of the information in Gopherspace even though the information is distributed over many different servers. Clients can either navigate through a hierarchy of directories and documents or ask an index server to return a list of all documents and directories that contain one or more keywords. The Gopher server presents information in a menu system that lets clients access Internet resources by subject. The typical Gopher client presents users with a directory hierarchy to navigate, and each directory may contain documents, other directories, and search programs. The items in the Gopher directory have both a content type associated with them and a name displayed to the user.

The Gopher Client Side

The type of Internet access account and the client program used affect the way users work with Gopher. The millions of users that have shell or menu accounts with service providers see a Gopher interface similar to the one shown in Figure 8.1. Recently, non-IP client programs have been appearing with graphical front-ends that are giving a mass audience access to Gopher sources. In addition, online services, such as America Online, are offering an Internet gateway with a graphical interface to Gopher servers to open up Gopherspace to an even wider audience. Figure 8.2 shows the America Online Gopher client.

FIGURE 8.1
A Gopher site as it appears using a shell account from a service provider

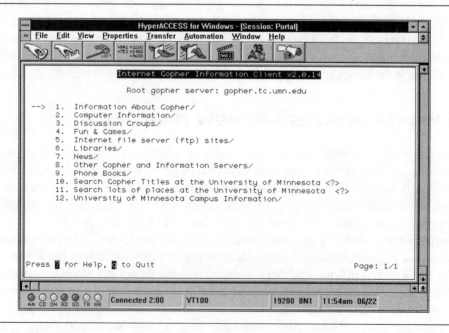

FIGURE 8.2

America Online's Gopher client

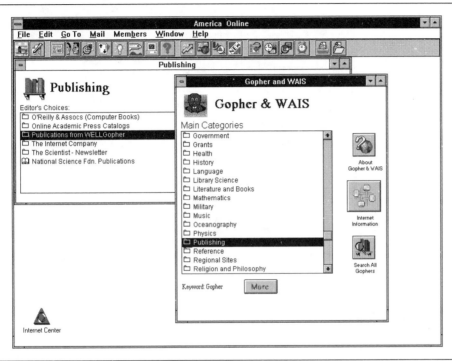

Internet users who have IP connections working with Gopher have an even more friendly interface and more features. Several free Gopher clients are available. Each Gopher client displays information a little differently. For example, some clients restrict the user to viewing each successive directory in a single window, and other clients display a different window for each directory. One of the most commonly used Windows Gopher clients is WsGopher. WinGopher is a commercial Gopher client that includes an impressive image viewer and a Telnet tool. WinGopher also provides top-notch technical support. Figure 8.3 shows the WinGopher client program. On the Macintosh side, the reigning Gopher program is TurboGopher (Figure 8.4). For more information on Gopher clients, see the appendix under "Internet Tools Software."

FIGURE 8.3

A Gopher site as it appears in the WinGopher client program

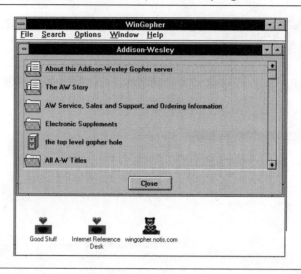

FIGURE 8.4

A Gopher site as it appears in the TurboGopher client program

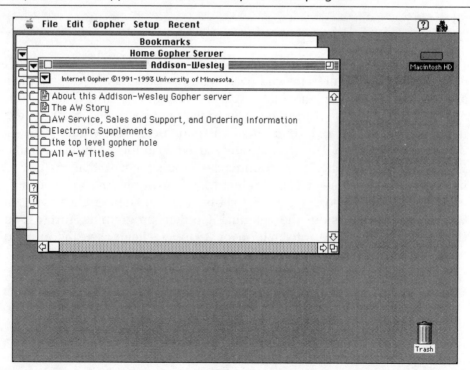

The Server Side of Gopher

Gopher serves UNIX, Windows, and Macintosh platforms. The most popular Gopher server for PCs is PC_Server. Mac_server for the Macintosh includes both the Gopher Surfer and the Gopher+ Mac server. The most popular Gopher server overall is Gopherd for UNIX. In addition, secure versions of Telnet and More called SecureGopher work with Gopher servers. Gopher servers also support WAIS indexing, so most servers also use WAIS to index Gopher information and data so it can be searched by Gopher clients.

Gopher+: The Next Generation

Like most Internet protocols, Gopher is evolving. The newest Gopher protocol is called Gopher+ and brings Gopher into the age of multimedia. Gopher+ lets Gopher servers include Microsoft Word, PostScript, RTF, and ASCII text versions of a single document that can be viewed online with Gopher+ clients. Gopher+ servers and clients let Gopher users work with different multimedia files online, including automatically displaying GIF and JPEG format image files, playing WAV and SND format sound files, and running MPEG and QuickTime video files.

Another big benefit of the Gopher+ protocol is the addition of attributes. *Attributes* are additional information associated with Gopher files. For example, Gopher+ may include a different icon for a PostScript file than an ASCII text file. For an image file, an icon can identify whether the file is in GIF or JPEG format. Thus, a Gopher+ client can automatically invoke the appropriate application to view or play the file.

Gopher+ also supports the *Ask Processing* feature, which lets a Gopher item present an interactive form or dialog box for the user to fill in. This allows servers to include a forms interface for performing business transactions. For example, a customer can fill out a form, click a Send button to send the form to the server, and have the server send the information, such as an online publication, directly to the client program. Figure 8.5 shows a sample of a Gopher+ form.

Another important feature of Gopher+ is authentication support, which allows access to information to be granted on an individual basis. Interestingly, the password is never sent across the network. However, this security system requires that both the server and the client know a password. The server picks a random number and uses the client's password to encrypt the number, then sends the encrypted number to the client so the client can decrypt the number. The client then increments the number by 1,

FIGURE 8.5

A Gopher+ form

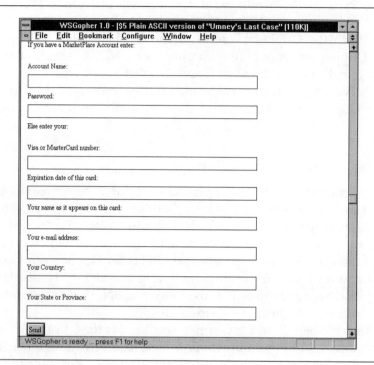

encrypts the new number, and sends it to the server. The server lets the user get access to the secured information. Because of limitations in using this type of authentication, it's likely that encryption schemes or other security mechanisms will replace it in future editions of Gopher.

A Day in the Life of a Gopher User

Internet users with shell or menu accounts can run a Gopher client from the service provider's computer or use the Telnet program to remotely log into a Gopher server. Once they're connected, they can work with Gopher. Internet users with IP connections can use a client program that makes the connection for them in the background.

Regardless of the way users connect to Gopherspace, the interface is simple enough that they can easily navigate the database of sites and quickly find the product or service information of interest. The interface guides the user from one screen to the next until the desired product information is delivered. Each Gopher host has a hierarchical menu of resources of special interest to that location, which is instantly accessible to the Internet user with a click or a keystroke.

To guide Gopher users through Gopherspace, several supporting search and index tools are commonly used. Veronica has become the most popular Gopher search program. It finds the Gopher servers most likely to contain useful information about a particular topic based on keywords the user specifies. Veronica asks the user for words to search for and builds a custom menu from the Gopher servers with menu items matching the keyword search. Veronica can search by menu items and directories or by directories only. Veronica also allows users to perform Boolean searches, so the user can use the words *and*, *or*, and *not* to control the search. A newer index program is JUG-HEAD (Jonzy's Universal Gopher Hierarchy Excavation and Display), which lets Gopher users limit searches to specific Gopher servers. Gopher also lets people use WAIS databases and utilities to find information and data.

A Gopher user looking for flowers could search Gopherspace using keywords such as *flowers* and *florist*, or if you knew the Gopher address of a florist, you could point your Gopher client directly to that site. For example, to go to Grant's Florist & Greenhouse, you can connect directly to the Gopher server at *branch.com*. The Branch Information Services mall appears, as shown in Figure 8.6. From the mall, the WinGopher user double-clicks on the Grant's FTD Flowers on the Internet icon to display the listing of files available. Double-click on the Ordering Flowers text file icon (Figure 8.7) to display the text information (Figure 8.8), and double-click on the Classic Dozen Red Roses icon to display the picture of an arrangement (Figure 8.9). Double-click on the Flower Order Form to display the order form (Figure 8.10).

FIGURE 8.6
The Branch Information Services mall

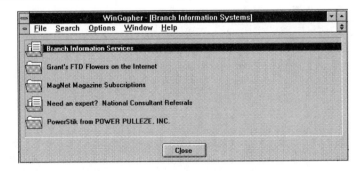

FIGURE 8.7

Grant's FTD Flowers on the Internet Gopher site

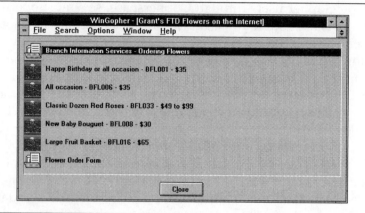

FIGURE 8.8

Ordering Flowers text file

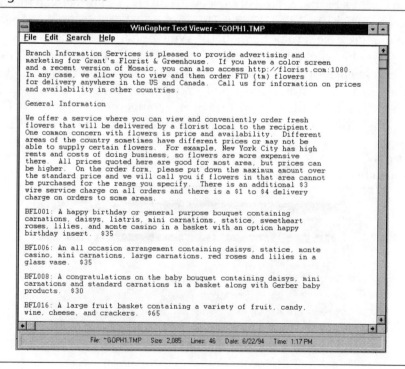

FIGURE 8.9
All occasion arrangement picture

FIGURE 8.10
Flower Order Form display

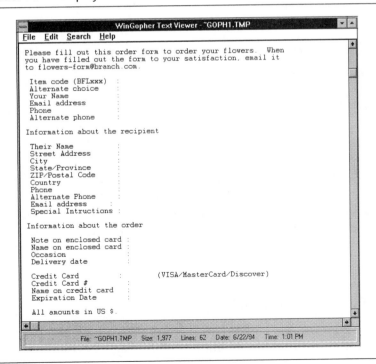

❏ ESTABLISHING A BUSINESS PRESENCE IN GOPHERSPACE

Gopherspace offers two key opportunities for a business. First, marketing with Gopher accesses the largest number of Internet users. Most people who have access to the Internet can use Gopher, and a growing number of commercial online services, such as America Online and Delphi, are offering access to Gopher. According to *Boardwatch Magazine,* the number of Gopher users grew by 997 percent between December 1993 and March 1994. On the server side, the number of Gopher servers grew from 4,800 to 6,700 between December 1993 and March 1994.

The second key opportunity for businesses is that Internet users can easily find your site. As with any retail business, it doesn't matter how great your product and services are if your customers can't find you. The ability to search all of Gopherspace by keywords makes it easier for Internet users to find your site.

On the negative side, the presentation of information in Gopher is somewhat clunky because information is always broken down into files. This means that Gopher users open a different file for text, pictures, and other media instead of viewing an integrated page of elements. However, if Adobe's Acrobat or other cross-platform document file formats become a standard, this could change.

❏ DETERMINING THE TYPE OF GOPHER PRESENCE FOR YOUR BUSINESS

Publishing and virtual storefronts are the two ways to establish your business presence using Gopher. Most server services operate electronic malls, where they list the businesses that have a presence at their site. The server service acts like a retail mall-management company that takes care of technical details of setting up, maintaining, and promoting your Gopher presence. Whether you're publishing information or creating a virtual storefront, your Gopher presence is usually part of the mall. The mall has the advantage of combining several businesses at one location to draw in a larger base of Internet users. The following sections give some examples of Gopher online publishing and Gopher storefronts.

Gopher Online Publishing

Online publishing is the easiest and least expensive option for establishing a Gopher presence. The cost of online publishing can run from a few hundred to several thousand dollars, depending on what you want to do. For example, you might publish a newsletter, provide a catalog, announce a new product, or list prices for your products and services. A good example of online publishing is the Electronic Newsstand, which was founded in July 1993 by The Internet Company, a server service company. The Electronic Newsstand provides the Internet community with easy access to a wide range of interesting information furnished by the world's leading magazine publishers. Like traditional newsstands, the Electronic Newsstand is a place where you can browse—for free—through many publications and have your interest stimulated by a variety of subjects. The newsstand provides a window on the world of computers, technology, science, business, foreign affairs, the arts, travel, medicine, nutrition, sports, politics, literature, and many other areas.

Every newsstand publisher provides the table of contents and several articles from each current issue. Users can order single copies or subscriptions to the printed versions of any of the publications they find on the Electronic Newsstand via e-mail or a special 800 number. Figure 8.11 shows the results of going to The Internet Company's server (internet.com) using WinGopher and choosing the Electronic Newsstand option.

FIGURE 8.11
The Electronic Newsstand

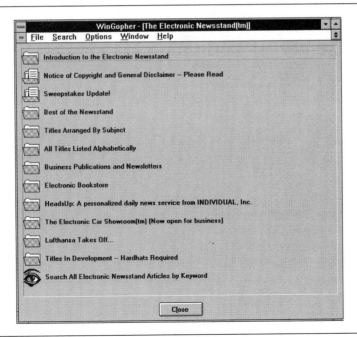

A Gopher Storefront

Setting up a virtual storefront to conduct online transactions is more complex and expensive than publishing because the service provider must create the infrastructure for handling the transactions. The server service will charge various fees to process orders and keep your virtual storefront running. The Online Bookstore (OBS) is a virtual storefront at Marketplace.com, an electronic mall run by Cyberspace Development. OBS has become a working model for operating a virtual storefront that sells online publishing. It pays royalties to authors and electronic rights holders for the titles they make available online. The OBS supports the Gopher+ protocol, so users can place Visa or MasterCard orders online to purchase the items for sale. Figure 8.12 shows Online Bookstore at CyberSpace Development's Marketplace (marketplace.com).

FIGURE 8.12
The Online Bookstore

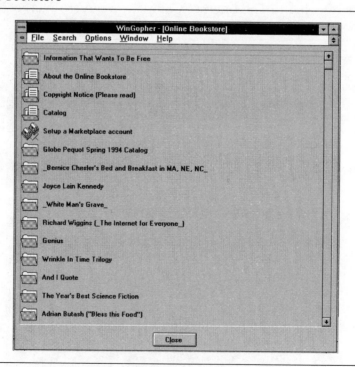

OBS offers online documents in a few different ways. They can be purchased per copy, as a site license, or as a subscription for a certain amount of time. Cyberspace Development and OBS handle order information in the strictest confidence. Neither company sells or otherwise shares customer information. A unique aspect of OBS is that if you have any comments or complaints, you can send mail directly to the Gopher site at *OBS@marketplace.com*. OBS also offers bound books as well as online documents. The titles available from OBS in text format via Gopher range from *Selected Poems* and *Hotel Lautreamont* by John Ashbery to the *Multimedia Law Handbook* by Dianne Brinson and Mark Radcliffe.

OBS also includes books in the Voyager Expanded Book format, which is a HyperCard format that can include illustrations and provides hypertext links so you can easily move around the document. The books in the Voyager Expanded Book format range from Madeleine L'Engle's *Wrinkle in Time* trilogy to *Sex: An Oral History* by Harry Maurer, published by Viking/Penguin in 1994. OBS also offers books in HTML format that use Mosaic as the reader (see Chapter 9 for more information on HTML and Mosaic).

One of OBS's most successful product rollouts was its 1993 prerelease to Internet readers of "Umney's Last Case," the story Stephen King liked best in his book *Nightmares and Dreamscapes.* OBS advertised the Internet release of the short story and gave readers three file format options for retrieving the text, which they could download or have mailed from Gopher. Additional files, including reviews, a Stephen King bibliography, and text from the book's foreword that explained why "Umney's Last Case," was Stephen King's favorite story, were offered at no charge. After the book was published in October 1993, OBS added two book reviews to the online files.

❑ DESIGNING AND SETTING UP YOUR GOPHER PRESENCE

Creating a Gopher presence involves determining what kind of information and services you want to offer Gopher users, designing your presence, and setting up your Gopher site using a server service. To create and set up a Gopher presence, you must understand the basic factors that affect the cost and operation of the Gopher site. For example, you need to know how many documents you want to present, what file formats you want to present them in, and approximately how much disk space is needed. Determining these factors will help you in working with the server service. The following sections walk you through the process of designing and setting up a Gopher business presence.

Determining What Information and Files You Want to Provide

The first stage in establishing a Gopher presence is determining what information you want to present to Gopher users, and in what file formats. To get an idea of how you want to present your business in Gopherspace, look at existing sites established by other businesses. This allows you to see what businesses are putting in their Gopher sites and what file formats they're using. As you think about defining your Gopher presence, you should consider the following:

- What information do you want to provide about your company?

- Do you want to provide information about one or more products?

- Do you want to provide a way for potential customers to order more information about your company or products?

- Do you want to sell software or information that can be delivered over the Internet?

In most cases, your Gopher presence will be a collection of files. Publishing information in a text format ensures that anyone on the Internet will be able to read it. However, ASCII text limits you from including any graphics and formatting, such as using bold and italic text in different sizes. To publish documents that include graphics and formatting, you can include a document in one or more of the following formats:

- PostScript files limit who can read your message, because the reader has to have a PostScript reader or a PostScript printer. PostScript readers and printers are common on the UNIX and Macintosh, but they are not as popular with IBM PCs and compatibles.

- Rich text format (RTF) is readable in most word processors, regardless of platform. The biggest limitation is that the document can contain only formatted text; it doesn't allow you to include graphic images.

- Picture files, such as files in GIF and JPEG format, require the reader to have a viewer or graphics program to display the picture file.

- Macintosh DiskPaper format converts Macintosh documents into stand-alone applications. This is especially useful for distributing documents created by graphic or presentation software.

- Adobe Acrobat PDF (portable document format) allows documents to be shared across platforms and promises to be a standard.

Virtually any document can be converted into a PDF file. Figure 8.13 shows a document presented in the Adobe Acrobat Reader.

- Common Ground files can be stored and read on different platforms. Common Ground lets you share formatted document files with different platforms. A Common Ground document includes a viewer program that automatically loads the document. Common Ground makes files available for the PC platforms: (DOS/ Windows), and Macintosh. Figure 8.14 shows a document in the Common Ground Viewer.

- HyperCard is a Macintosh hypertext and database program. HyperCard files, called HyperCard stacks, are usually stored in a compressed format, typically using the StuffIt compression program (identified by the extension .sit).

- HTML stands for HyperText Markup Language, which is used to create World-Wide Web documents that can be viewed by Mosaic or other Web browser. See Chapter 9 for more information on the World-Wide Web, Mosaic, and HTML.

FIGURE 8.13
A document in the Adobe Acrobat Reader

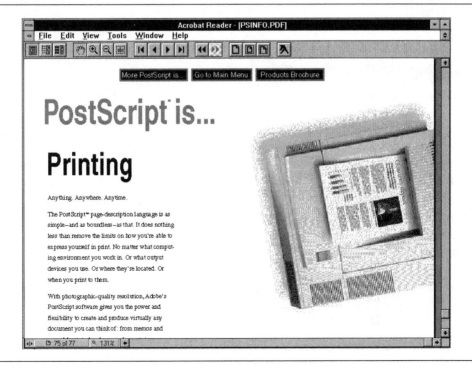

FIGURE 8.14
A document in the Common Ground Reader

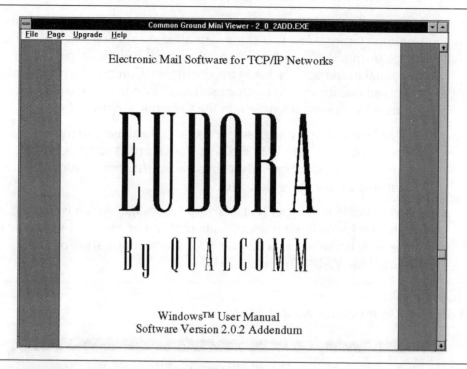

Defining Attributes and Keywords

Having a product or service available is successful only if people can find it. You should identify *classifications* and *attributes* to let Gopher users find your product or service using keywords that you choose. When choosing keywords, keep in mind that keyword searches are case-insensitive.

Classifications are a set of goods or services with comparable attributes. Think of this index as you would the categories you'd find in the classified ads section of your local newspaper or the index to businesses you might find in a telephone directory. Classifications narrow a search. A classification index is a permuted index so that, for instance, when users specify the keyword *books*, it might match *books, Online Bookstore,* and *authors*.

Attributes help Gopher users locate the information they want. Say, for example, you wanted to create an entry for a travel agency so information is available to anyone looking up the keywords *travel, transportation, trip, tickets* and *cruise*. It's up to you, not the server service, to define the attribute names associated with your product or service. Each attribute can take on a value; for example, a *location* might be *Bahamas* and *class*, might be *coach.*

Be sure to give the server service a description of your goods or services and identify any names commonly used to refer to your product or service. A server service typically lists numerous entries in the database to identify your product or service. You can list as many or as few goods or services as you like; however, you typically must file a separate form for each product description or attribute set you would like to appear on the system.

Defining Connections to Other Internet Resources

Gopher is intertwined with other Internet tools, so Gopher users visiting your site can link to other Internet resources. For example, you can customize Gopher menus and pointers to do any of the following:

- Search the Archie database to locate files on the Internet (see Chapter 7 for more on Archie)

- Use Telnet to log into a remote system or online library

- Access other Gopher servers around the world

- Read or download online documents

- Access local WAIS databases and indexes to locate information

- Query remote WAIS databases and indexes, and funnel the results to Gopher clients

- Query remote FTP sites, and send the results to Gopher clients

- Be queried by Web clients using either built-in Gopher querying or HTTP querying

- Download files, including binary and encoded files, such as image and sound files

- Access HTML (hypertext markup language) data (HTML is the language used to present Web information)

Working with a Gopher Server Service

A good server service will have experience from performing similar functions for other businesses. This lets your business focus on your products and services and leaves the technical details of operating a Gopher site to the server service. Prices and services vary widely between server services, so make sure you do some serious shopping. Because various charges are associated with establishing a Gopher site, you need to define what you want as clearly as you can, so you can get an accurate quote. Keep the following general guidelines in mind as you look for a server service to set up a Gopher presence.

- Does the server service have the big enough connection bandwidth to support a high volume of Gopher traffic? (at least a full T1)

- How much does the server service charge for a setup fee, and how much is the monthly fee? Is the monthly fee fixed?

- How much does the server service charge for disk space? Most server services assess an additional charge for each megabyte of space in excess of 100,000 bytes (roughly 25 to 50 pages of text).

- Will the server service set up both Gopher and Telnet sites that list goods or services?

- How does the server service charge your business? Many server services retain a percentage of the gross sales of the storefront, much like malls do for their retail tenants.

- What are the server service's billing terms? If you are an established firm, some server services will honor standard billing terms: 30 days net. Nonrated firms and individuals need to pay by check, money order, or credit card.

- In what format does the server service require the text and graphics you want to present on the Gopher site's listing of products and services? You can usually send your company's product or service description file via e-mail, usually up to 100,000 bytes (characters) long. In most cases, keep your description as close to a screenful of text as possible or break your message into multiple smaller messages, so you don't overwhelm your readers.

- What rules and restrictions apply to your Gopher site postings? Different service providers and server services have different rules and restrictions. Because advertising on the Internet is not regulated, it is important that you read all information the server service submits for installation on the net.

- What is the server service liable for? For example, what happens if the server is down? Do you still have to pay? What happens if your marketing materials are damaged as a result of the server service's installation or maintenance, or by someone accessing the server? Most server services are offered as is, with no warranties of any kind. You should not depend on a service provider for any high-risk activities that require fail-safe performance, or products and services in which defects in or failure of materials could cause personal injury, loss of property, or environmental damage. Remember that copyright laws apply to text posted on the net. Any information you post is in the public domain. Most server services include disclaimers to protect them from liability, since other users might unintentionally include text that violates any other party's proprietary rights.

- Does the server service support Gopher+? Gopher+ is especially beneficial if you're planning to use forms for credit-card transactions.

- How much does the server service charge to update existing entries? Usually, you can update an existing entry at little or no charge, unless updates exceed once per month.

- Does the server service also provide BBS support? A BBS (bulletin board system) lets any user with a modem order products or services.

Handling Gopher Business Transactions

Server services can handle Gopher transactions in a variety of ways. If you're creating a storefront that will take credit cards, the service provider typically charges for each credit-card transaction and/or order notification. You need your own business credit-card merchant account. Many server services let you choose from a wide variety of customer pricing and charging options. For example, you can charge your storefront customers by item (per file, per document), access (per connection with no time limit), connection time, subscription (individual, site, or company), search (regardless of success of search), or hit (fee for each successful search result).

Using Gopher+ lets a server service minimize risk by allowing customers to enter their credit-card information once via a form and then choose a unique account name and password. When a customer wants to make a purchase from any vendor on the net, he or she just provides the account name which is used to locate the credit-card information. (A confirmation password is also required.)

❏ PROMOTING YOUR GOPHER PRESENCE

You should budget for several months of operation to allow time for word to spread about your Gopher site. Some server services provide their own advertising to draw business. Choosing an active server service can also bring new business, since you may be able to draw customers from the marketing activities of the other vendors. Your Gopher site will show up in all Gopher directories and in all searches initiated by potential customers.

In addition to what the server service does to promote its Gopher site, you can promote your Gopher presence in other ways. Chapter 4 explains the general promotional options available on the Internet. Here are several specific ways to promote your Gopher presence:

- See if you can have a link added to your Gopher from another Gopher server. Several Gopher sites include links to commercial businesses, such as the Well's Gopher (put together by Eric Theise) and CyberSpace Development's Marketplace (Andrew Currie), and the Internet Shopping Mall (put together by Dave Taylor).

- Once your Gopher site is set up, you can have the site appear as part of the Other Gophers hierarchy by sending mail to *Gopher@boombox.micro.umn.edu.* You can do this as part of the setup by your server service, so ask your server service first.

- You can have your Gopher site added to the Gopher Jewels catalog, which is a listing of Gopher sites by category. Gopher Jewels is a moderated list service with over 1,500 subscribers, whose purpose is to share interesting Gopher sites. You can ask to have your site added by sending mail to the list moderator, *david.riggins@ tpoint.com.* Your post should explain why the Gopher site is worth visiting, and be sure to include the Gopher site's name and host address.

Chapter 9

Multimedia Marketing with the World-Wide Web

The newest and fastest-growing Internet tool is the World-Wide Web. This slick multimedia Internet tool lets users access resources in a rich environment of hypertext links, graphics, fonts, sound, video, and more. World-Wide Web and friendly, graphical-based clients like Mosaic are changing the face of the Internet. For businesses, establishing a World-Wide Web presence—from a simple advertisement to a full-service virtual storefront—is staking a claim on the future of the Internet. The good news is businesses can affordably get started right now. This chapter explains how any business can take advantage of the explosive marketing opportunities of the World-Wide Web.

❑ WHAT IS WORLD-WIDE WEB, AND HOW DOES IT WORK?

World-Wide Web, commonly referred to as the Web (also called WWW or W3) was developed at CERN (European Laboratory for Particle Physics) in Switzerland. The protocol that forms the foundation of the Web is Hypertext Transport Protocol (HTTP). The Web is a client/server system. Internet users with IP access typically use a client program, commonly called a *browser*, that runs in their native environment to access Web servers (or other types of Internet servers such as FTP or Gopher). A Web document is a text document created using the hypertext markup language (HTML). HTML is a coding system for making hypertext links and sending formatted text and graphics from Web servers to Web browsers.

Any Web document can contain links to other documents and resources. These links are based on an addressing scheme called universal resource locator (URL). Linked references within a Web document or list become the jumping-off points to other documents, lists, resources, or actions. Pools of

143

information become joined into a centralized graphical document that lets users follow references by selecting highlighted keywords and items. The Web relates to existing resources in a simple manner by pointing to the specific resource target. The target can be a text file, an image, a specific part of a text file, a Gopher server, an FTP site, or various other types of information. For example, an Internet user can click on highlighted hypertext in a Web document that links the user to a file stored at an FTP or Gopher site.

The work of locating and displaying the target information is done within the local Web client application. All that is transferred across the Internet is the information, which is displayed according to the settings and built-in rules of the browser. All formatting and layout information is constructed locally, according to the client software and preference settings. Figure 9.1 shows a sample HTML-coded document, and Figure 9.2 shows how it appears in the PC version of Mosaic. Figure 9.3 shows how another document appears in MacWeb on the Macintosh.

FIGURE 9.1
A Web document with its HTML codes

FIGURE 9.2

A Web document as it appears in Mosaic on the PC

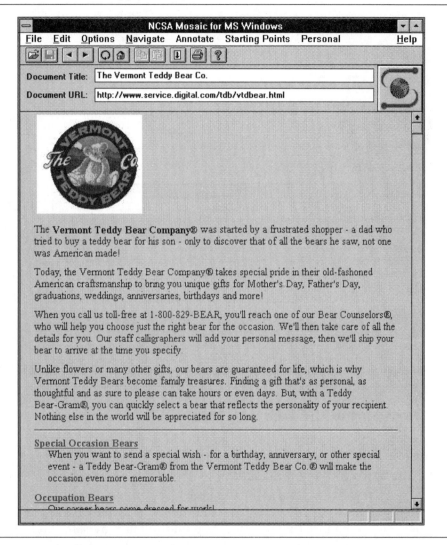

FIGURE 9.3
A Web document as it appears in MacWeb on the Macintosh

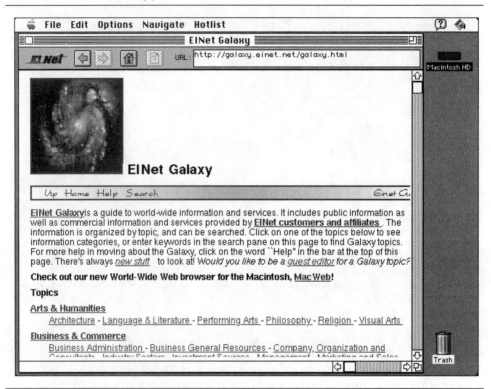

The Client Side of the Web

Although the Web has been in existence for over four years, in 1993 its use exploded across the Internet. Much of the credit for this sudden popularity can be attributed to the graphical World-Wide Web client program Mosaic. Mosaic was created by the National Center for Supercomputing Applications (NCSA) at the University of Illinois at Urbana-Champaign. The National Science Foundation, a key U.S. government player in the Internet, funded the NCSA Mosaic effort. You can obtain Mosaic free of charge by downloading it from NCSA. For information on how to get a copy of Mosaic from NCSA, see the appendix under "Internet Tools Software." Mosaic is available for Windows, Macintosh, and X Windows platforms. Mosaic runs in conjunction with TCP/IP software. For example, on a Windows PC, a user might be running Chameleon as the TCP/IP software, and a Mac might be running MacTCP. Once an Internet connection is established, the user installs and runs the Mosaic program.

With all the success Mosaic has had, it's little wonder that other Web client programs are appearing. Netcom includes a Web browser as part of its NetCruiser software, which is bundled with a Netcom connection. EINet's MacWeb client, which is a browser for the Macintosh, is an impressive browser. Other browsers, such as Cello, are available, but they are not as sophisticated as Mosaic, MacWeb, and Netcom's NetCruiser. Many companies are licensing Mosaic to create their own interface to the Web. For example, Quarterdeck Office Systems and Spry Inc. have licensed the source code for Mosaic from NCSA to introduce commercial versions of Mosaic that will include enhancements and technical support. Other players are sure to follow.

One of the benefits of Mosaic is that it provides a uniform interface across platforms. Mosaic generally works the same way regardless of the platform. However, the X Windows version of Mosaic is the primary development platform, so XMosaic features are likely to be included in the Windows and Mac versions.

Web browsers support multimedia extensions for fonts, digitized images, video clips, sound files, and more. Web browsers support a number of external programs to display digitized images, view video clips, and play sound files. The most common multimedia formats currently found on the World-Wide Web are:

- For graphics, GIF (Graphics Interchange Format), JPEG (Joint Photographic Experts Group), and XBM (X BitMaps)

- For sound, Audio (AU), Waveform (WAV), and Sound (SND)

- For video, MPEG (Motion Picture Experts Group), Microsoft Video for Windows (AVI), and QuickTime

Viewers for files in these formats are available for X Windows, Microsoft Windows, and Macintosh. Clients may also support additional machine-specific formats.

Web browsers can do more than view Mosaic documents and files; they can also perform many other Internet tasks. For example, using a Web browser like Mosaic lets users do any of the following:

- Access Gopher sites and perform searches with Veronica

- Search for files using an Archie request form

- Transfer files from FTP sites

- Use Telnet to go to other computers

- Use the Finger and Whois gateways to get site and user information

The Server Side of the Web

The real strength of Web client software is when users connect to a Web server. Users can then work with information in a graphical user interface (GUI) and link to all kinds of other Internet resources. NCSA developed the HTTD Web server that is currently the dominant Web server software. The HTTD server is a simple program that basically supports Mosaic clients by sending HTML commands to the client software on demand. Mac and Windows versions of Web server software include the NCSA server, CERN server, MacHTTP, HTTPS for Windows NT, and SerWeb.

The Future of the Web and Mosaic

The Web and browsers are constantly improving, with expanded capabilities. The expansion of Web has been phenomenal so far, and its future looks even more promising. As ISDN and leased lines become less expensive, video and sound are sure to become commonplace. As more standard file formats are supported, it is likely to improve the symbiotic relationship needed between the HTTP servers and browsers. Right now facilities are added to the HTTP server software are not always immediately reflected in the Mosaic client, and Mosaic is adding facilities that not all HTTP servers are capable of servicing. Some of the new features that are being incorporated in the Macintosh and Windows versions of Mosaic include the following:

- Better form support. This is a biggie because it offers a front-end to many other services such as databases and search engines.

- Interactive forms feature, with the ability to include text-entry areas, toggle buttons, selection lists, and pop-up menus. The combination of interactive forms with formatted text, graphics, hypermedia links, and the ability to launch a separate application insures that Mosaic will become the front-end for other interactive services. Interactive forms can be used to submit order forms, provide front-end interfaces to databases and search engines, register for membership online, gather user comments and suggestions, and register votes for favorite movies.

- Ability to authenticate the identity of users by user name and password. Once a user is authenticated on a server, Mosaic should be able to reuse the information without asking for it again.

- Provide direct WAIS access. Mosaic will be able to talk directly to WAIS servers and handle data that is retrieved, including graphic images and audio and video files.

- Ability to launch external processes via hyperlinks—viewers, sound players, MIME file mapping.

- Make transparent URL redirections. If a server returns a pointer to another document, Mosaic will then attempt to reach the new destination without showing the intermediate step to the user.

- Remote control features, such as mouse tracking to interact with maps or other graphics.

A Day in the Life of a Web User

When a user starts a browser, the document window displays a *home page.* For example, starting Mosaic automatically displays NCSA's home page. You can customize the browser to default to any Web server's home page. This home page is the starting point for users to navigate the Web. From the home page, users can click on highlighted text or graphic objects to make links to other Web documents or Internet tool servers, depending on what is offered on the particular home page.

A Web document can contain text and pictures, some of which are hypertext links, called *anchors,* to other documents or resources. These links can be highlighted or underlined, or inline images can have anchors associated with them so they will appear with a thin colored line around them. Users can point their Mosaic client to any Web server by entering an address in the URL field. URL is a system of identifying where a resource resides on the Internet. To point to a particular home page on a Web server, users enter a unique URL address. For example, users entering http//www.novell.com in the URL field will point Mosaic to Novell's Web home page, as shown in Figure 9-4.

FIGURE 9.4

The Web home page for Novell

On the Novell home page, users can point and click on any of the books on the shelf to view that specific information. For example, clicking on the What's New volume leads to a page of information about new developments at Novell. The browser lets users navigate deeper into the links, return step by step to the home page, or move to another home page. Web users can maintain hot lists so they can quickly return to the Web sites they want. Figures 9.5 and 9.6 show the Internet Shopping Network home page and the results of clicking on a hypertext reference.

FIGURE 9.5
The Internet Shopping Network (ISN) home page

FIGURE 9.6
The result of clicking on a hypertext link in ISN home page

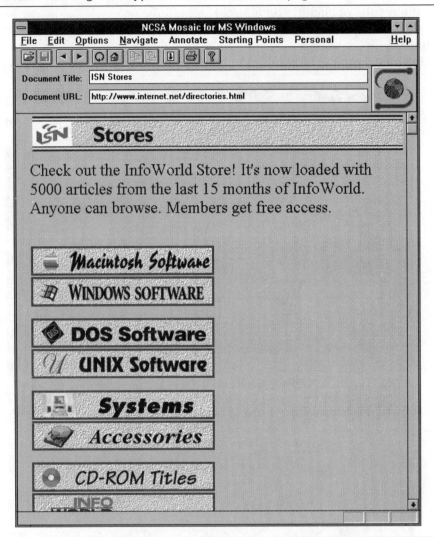

❑ DETERMINING THE TYPE OF WEB PRESENCE FOR YOUR BUSINESS

Establishing a Web presence is an exciting and powerful way to present your business on the Internet. Because the Web is such a versatile tool, businesses can choose from a wide variety of options, ranging from publishing a single display advertisement or brochure to a full-service virtual storefront.

The beauty of setting up a Web presence is that your business can start out small with just an advertisement; it can then expand as your Internet-generated business increases. Establishing a Web server presence is a multi-faceted process that includes determining the scope of your presence, and designing, creating, and setting up your presence with the right server service. One guiding principle to keep in mind when establishing a Web presence is that you must dedicate the resources to design an effective visual presentation that organizes and links information, using copyedited text and quality graphics.

Most server services operate electronic malls where they list the businesses that have a presence at their site. The server service acts like a retail mall-management company that takes care of technical details of setting up, maintaining, and promoting your Web presence. Whether you're publishing a simple brochure or an information center, or creating a virtual storefront, it is part of the mall. Users can access your Web document either by starting at the server services home page or by moving directly to your home page via its unique URL address. The mall has the advantage of combining multiple businesses at one location to draw in a larger base of Internet users. Additionally, the server service promotes the mall site on the Internet.

FYI

See Chapter 4 for information on working with server services in general. For a listing of server services, see the appendix.

Single-Page Brochure

Publishing a single-page brochure is the easiest and least expensive option for establishing a Web presence. Many server services let you set up a single-page brochure for less than a few hundred dollars a year. A simple brochure might include a single picture, such as a logo, text, and a link to another Internet resource. The link might be to a file you have at an anonymous FTP site or any other resource on the Internet. A good example of a brochure is Michele~Shine media, which is found in the InterNex electronic mall (Figure 9.7). Michele~Shine media is a multimedia design company, based in San Francisco, that offers a full range of design services including Web document design (see the appendix under "Web Design Services" for more information). Its Web brochure includes a logo, a description of what it does, and pictures of the two designers. It doesn't include any links, but it offers users a brochure of its services.

FIGURE 9.7
Michele~Shine media home page

An Information Center

A more sophisticated Web presence is an information center that includes multiple pages. For example, you might publish an online catalog that can include pictures of products, text, and icons. Internet users can browse through your catalog, then place orders through your existing order-fulfillment operation, such as an 800 number or even via e-mail. *Wired* is a new, hot magazine that merges the technical and design worlds. Its Web information-center presence is an extension of the published magazine. Figure 9.8 shows the home page of the *Wired* information resource center. Users can search articles by keywords (Figure 9.9) or read articles from the current issue.

FIGURE 9.8
Wired magazine home page

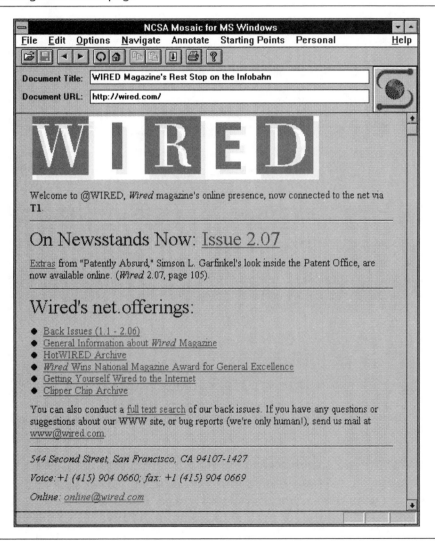

FIGURE 9.9

WAIS database to search *Wired* articles

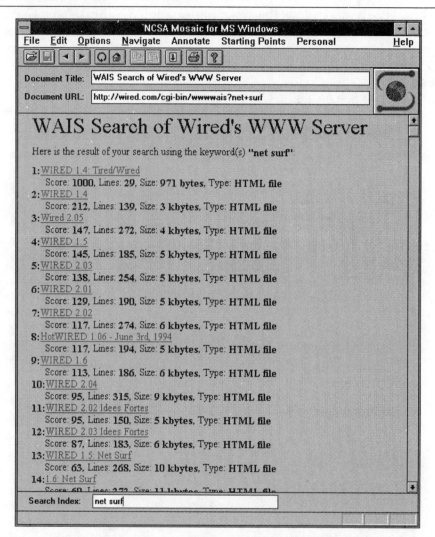

An even more sophisticated example of an information center comes from the *Palo Alto Weekly*, a community-based weekly newspaper serving several communities in Silicon Valley. The *Palo Alto Weekly* has established an extensive Web presence on an electronic mall operated by the Internet Distribution Service. Every week, a large part of the paper is put on the Web server, including the cover story, news, columns, sports, arts and entertain-

FIGURE 9.10

The *Palo Alto Weekly* home page

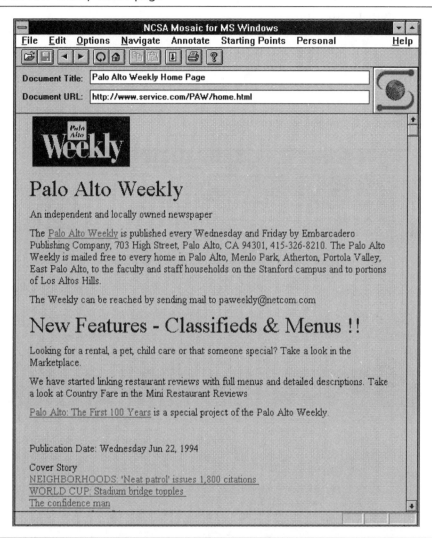

ment, dining and movie listings and reviews, and even classified ads. Figure 9.10 shows the home page of the *Palo Alto Weekly*.

A Virtual Storefront

A virtual storefront is more complex and expensive than an online brochure or an information center. Creating the infrastructure for handling transac-

157

tions requires a lot of customization by the server service. Additionally, the server service charges various fees to process transactions and keep your virtual storefront running.

An example of a virtual storefront is Grant's Florist & Greenhouse. A Mosaic user connects to the Branch Mall or uses the unique URL for Grant's Florist & Greenhouse. Figure 9.11 shows the home page for Grant's Florist &

FIGURE 9.11

Grant's Florist & Greenhouse home page

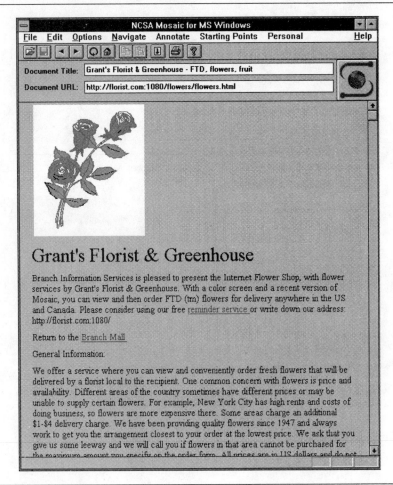

FIGURE 9.12
The list of flower arrangements

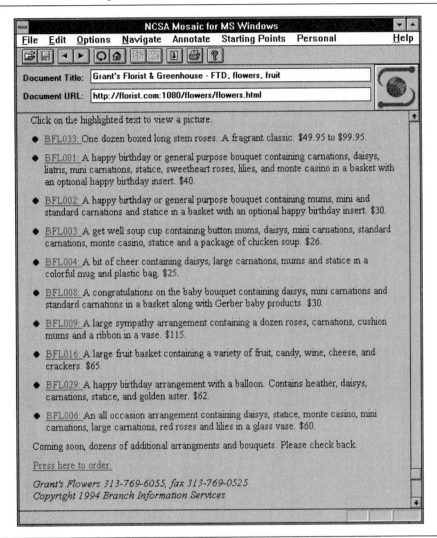

Greenhouse. The home page presents a list of flower arrangements (Figure 9.12), each of which is linked to another page containing a picture and more information about the arrangement (Figure 9.13). After you decide on an arrangement, you click on a hypertext link to display the Flowers Order Form (Figure 9.14).

FIGURE 9.13
A flower arrangement page

FIGURE 9.14
The form for ordering flowers

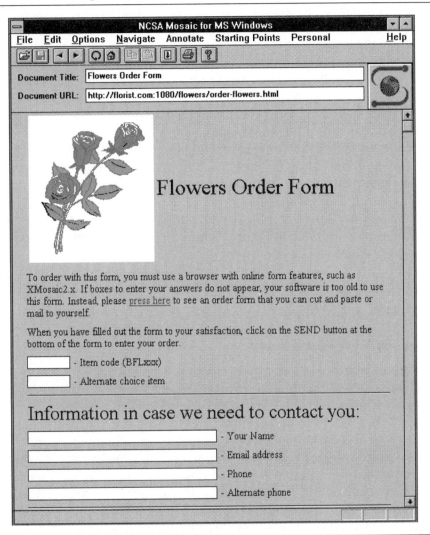

❑ DESIGNING AND SETTING UP A WEB PRESENCE

The process of creating and setting up a Web presence can be broken down into four stages. The first stage involves designing your Web presence. This involves understanding the basic factors that affect the cost and operation of the Web site balanced with the cost of designing and creating a professional-looking presence. For example, from designing your Web presence you can answer such questions as how many pages and links you want and the approximate disk space needed. You will also be in a better position to decide whether you want to provide server-ready copy or hire the server service to help create the copy.

The second stage involves assembling the pieces of your Web presence, which includes writing and copyediting text and creating the images you want to use in your Web documents.

The third stage is creating the actual Web document. You can script your own Web documents or hire a Web design service. Also, most server services will create an HTML document for you. The fee for creating a Web document usually ranges from $50 to $150 an hour. Even if the server service creates the document for you, you need to work out what you want to publish and in what type of layout. Keep in mind that many server services are run by technical people, not graphic designers. As a result, they can be familiar with the mechanics of creating an HTML document, but in most cases you won't get professional design input.

The final stage is working with a server service to set up your Web presence. The following section walks you through the process of establishing a Web business presence.

Designing Your Web Presence

The Web design process involves creating a layout for the text, graphics, links, and other elements you want to present. You can use desktop publishers, existing advertisements, or other resources to develop a layout, but be aware that many desktop publishing and advertising companies don't have experience designing Web documents. Your home page is the first impression an Internet user has of your business. As such, it's your most important starting point in terms of designing your Web presence. Your home page can contain formatted text, a scanned logo, related images, or sounds to describe your products or services. Many server service providers let you create links to other resources available at another site. For example, if you want to have files from an anonymous FTP site at your service provider, you can have a link established from your home page to a file. The Mosaic user can click on the hypertext to see the text in the file. If the file is in a format supported by the Web, it will be displayed as formatted. The following are some tips for designing an impressive Web presence.

- Study different Web sites using a browser to get ideas of how you might want to have your home page look and function.

- Determine what you want to publish and what you want to display, such as logos, links, graphics, sounds, and so on.

- Design your Web documents according to concepts. Organize your presentation, then match documents to it.

- Don't overuse graphics in your Web designs. If you lay out Web pages with large graphic images or use numerous graphics, your presentation will take a long time to be delivered to the browser. This is especially a problem for dial-up IP users.

- Think about how you want to present hyperlinks when designing your Web presence. For example, you may want to provide links tailored to different types of readers. Hypermedia provides a new generation of options for document design that are not available in linear, paper-based documents.

- Keep in mind that the more information and the fancier the presentation of your Web presence, the more expensive it will be. For example, many server services charge fees for the disk space your graphics and information take up.

- Manage the size of your text blocks. Long passages of text take longer to transfer, so a reader will not be able to quickly jump from long passages of text. It can be difficult for some readers with slower connections to scroll through large documents. Balance this with the fact that longer documents are easier to work with and print than documents with an excessive number of hyperlinks.

- Know your layout and formatting options as defined by HTML and HTML+. The HTML and HTML+ scripting language options and limitations are discussed later in this chapter.

- Ask your server service for guidelines for authoring Web documents. This will help to ensure a smooth transition from document to Web presence.

Creating the Pieces

The next step is to create the pieces needed for your Web presence. For example, write the text and scan or create pictures so you can put the pieces together by encoding them into an HTML document. Viewers are available for common World-Wide Web formats. GIF and JPEG files formats are popular in most UNIX, PC, and Macintosh graphic programs. XBM is an X Windows graphic format that is typically found on UNIX computers. Audio (AU) files are commonly created on UNIX systems. While programs exist for creating and playing Waveform (WAV) and Sound (SND) formats, most audio files are in AU format. If you are creating sound files on a PC or Mac, you may need a program to convert the sound file to the AU format. The MPEG, AVI, and QuickTime video file formats can be played on all platforms, but most video files on the Web are in the MPEG or QuickTime format. The following are general guidelines to keep in mind when creating the pieces of your Web presence.

- Create files in the formats that are supported by all versions of Mosaic. These are GIF (Graphics Interchange Format), JPEG (Joint Photographic Experts Group), XBM (X BitMaps), AU (Audio), MPEG (Motion Picture Experts Group), and QuickTime.

- Write content-based marketing text to attract Internet users to your Web site.

- Address the audience that will most frequently be accessing your Web document.

- Determine where information is coming from; for example, are you going to refer to or copy information?

- Have a copy editor edit your text.

Coding Web Documents

Behind every Web document is the source HTML code that brings the document to life after the browser receives the commands from the Web server. Web documents are created using hypertext markup language (HTML), which is a subset of SGML (standard general markup language). HTML commands, referred to as *tags,* are embedded within an ASCII text document known as a *source* document. You can use a word processor, text editor, or HTML editor to create source documents. HTML lets you lay out Web document formatting, such as the document title, section headers, character formatting, bulleted lists, inline images, and hypertext links.

Once you create a source document, you can open and view it within the browser to see what it will look like when it's placed on a Web server. For example, any Mosaic user can easily view the HTML coding behind any Web document simply by displaying the document and then choosing the Source Document command from the File menu in Mosaic. Once a document source is displayed, the user can choose to copy the source document by choosing the Copy command from the Edit menu. Figure 9.15 shows the

FIGURE 9.15
InterNex home page

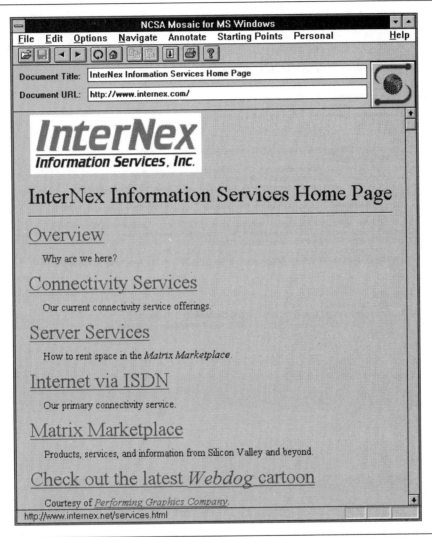

FIGURE 9.16
Source document for the InterNex home page

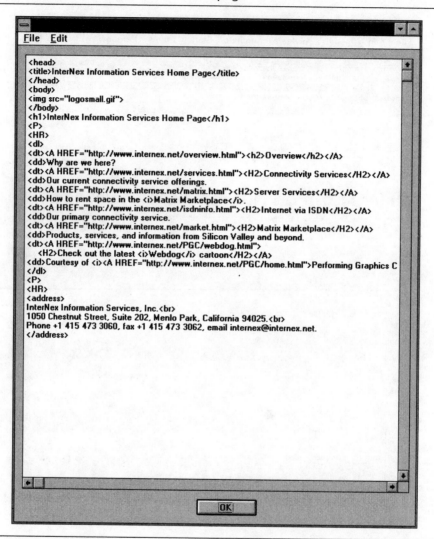

InterNex home page document in Mosaic, and Figure 9.16 shows the HTML source document for that home page.

HTML tags tell the browser how to lay out the text and also how to make links to other parts of documents. Using HTML commands, you can format a Web document to incorporate hypertext (and hypermedia), text in different fonts, character formatting (such as italic and boldface), and layout elements such as paragraphs, bulleted lists, quoted paragraphs, and more.

Compared to the power of desktop publishing capabilities, however, HTML is limited in its layout features. A new generation of HTML, called HTML+, is coming into use. It offers new enhancements to make more sophisticated Web documents. Some of the notable improvements include the following:

- Greater flexibility in specifying link destinations. Parts of an image will have separate links, providing a full hypermedia environment for such images as maps or annotated diagrams.

- The ability to create tables with titles and column headings, and an ability to let entries and headings span columns.

- Support for forms that allow users to query or update information sources and fill in questionnaires to be sent via e-mail and fax.

A Web client uses the tag information to format the text (and other media) for the viewer. HTML tags consist of a left angle bracket (<), followed by some text (called the *directive*) and closed by a right angle bracket (>). Tags are usually paired. The ending tag looks just like the starting tag, except a slash (/) precedes the text within the brackets. HTML is not case-sensitive: <title> is equivalent to <TITLE>. Typically, most Web designers use lowercase. Not all tags are supported by all browsers. If a browser doesn't support a tag, it ignores it.

HTML links text and images in an HTML document to other documents or images by way of HREFs (hypertext references), which are called *anchors*. These sections of text contain a pointer to another source. The browser highlights them, and clicking on them makes the jump to the source. Another important HTML tag is the inline image, which enables pictures to be included within the text of a document. A few HTML editors simplify creating HTML documents. Figure 9.17 shows the HyperEdit HTML editor for Windows, and Figure 9.18 shows the bbedit HTML editor for the Macintosh. See the appendix for a listing of HTML editors. Table 9.1 lists some of the most common HTML commands.

FIGURE 9.17

The HyperEdit Tool simplifies creating HTML documents

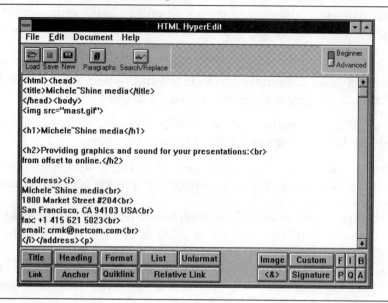

FIGURE 9.18

The bbedit HTML editor for the Macintosh

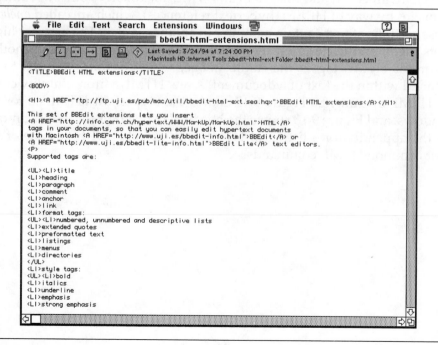

TABLE 9.1
Common HTML Commands and What They Do

Name	Tag and Description	Example
Title	<title> identifies the title of your Web document.	<title>Welcome to Bookware</title>
Headings	<h1>...<h6> indicate six levels of headings.	<h1>Recent Publications </h1>
Paragraphs	<p> instructs Mosaic to start a new paragraph and occurs only at the end of the paragraph.	This is a single paragraph. <p>
Line Breaks	 indicates a line break and forces text to start on a new line.	This text appears on one line. This text appears directly under the previous line.
Italic	<i> formats characters in italics. <cite> is used for citations such as the name of a book.	<I> It's Here!</i> <cite>The Internet Business Companion<cite>
Boldface	<b> formats characters in boldface.	<b> Important News </b>
Underlined Text	<u> identifies underlined text.	<u> Wired magazine </u>
Quote	<blockquote> indicates a section of text quoted from some other source.	<blockquote> Cybersurfing the Internet can be a wipeout for the uninitiated. </blockquote>
Preformatted Text	<pre> identifies text that has already been formatted by some other system, such as text in a fixed-width font.	<pre>The number to call is 967–0559</pre>

(continued on next page)

TABLE 9.1 (continued)
Common HTML Commands and What They Do

Name	Tag and Description	Example
Inline Images	<img src="*filename.gif*"> identifies the source of a graphics file. By default, the bottom of an image is aligned with the text. To align text with the top of the graphic image, add align=*top* to your inline image tag: <img align=top src= "*filename.gif*">	<img align=top src="logo.gif">
Horizontal Rules	<hr> creates a horizontal dividing line.	<hr>
HyperText Links	<a href="*filename.htm*"</a> indicates a hypertext link, where *a* stands for anchor.	<a href="*info.htm*"</a>
Unnumbered Lists	Unnumbered lists appear as bulleted lists. Unnumbered lists require two types of tags: <ul> heads the list, and <li> *list item* identifies each item.	<ul> <li>*Pens* <li>*Bookmarks* </ul>
Numbered List	Numbered lists, referred to as ordered lists, require <ol> at the beginning and end, and <li> *list item* identifes each list item.	<ol> <li> Do not pass go. <li> Do not collect $200. </ol>
Address	<address> specifies the author of a document and how to contact the author—usually, an e-mail address. Use to provide line breaks for each part of the address.	<address> info@bookware.com David Angell dangell@bookware.com Brent Heslop bheslop@bookware.com </address>

Working with a Web Server Service

Finding the right server service takes a concerted effort. Services and pricing are not uniform. Not taking the time and effort to shop for the right server service for setting up your Web presence can be an expensive mistake. Unfortunately, there isn't a *Consumer Reports* type of service for buyers of server services. The following guidelines can help you through the process of finding the right server service for establishing a Web presence.

- View the server service company's Web server. Check what Web documents it has done for other businesses. Check to make sure the documents look well-designed and professional.

- Check server service sites for information about server service options and pricing. Many publish their prices on their home page, and others deliver information using a mailbot. Or you may need to call the server service. Because many server services establish a Web presence for businesses on a case-by-case basis, many will not have a detailed menu of options and pricing.

- Ask if the server service will accept server-ready copy. Check also to see what type of price break you get when providing server-ready copy.

- Compare pricing across different server services using the same Web presence configuration. Don't assume that because a server service is expensive in one configuration, it'll be expensive in all configurations.

- Develop a budget for your commitment, and calculate the costs for every aspect of setting up the site: costs of creating the Web documents, storage costs, credit-card transaction charges, download charges, and consulting charges. Leave no stone unturned.

- Determine how your company will monitor the results of business generated from your Web presence. Find out if and how the server service tracks activity. Get a sample report to see if the information is useful as it's generated. If not, see if you can get a customized report.

- Find out how the server service is marketing its Web site on the Internet and in non-Internet publications. Because your home page is usually located in the server service's electronic mall, the mall site is promoted by the server service provider.

- Define what you need as specifically as possible before getting a quote. For example, what art do you want to include, in what format are you delivering your material, and how much information are you linking? These factors will affect your costs, because many server services charge for these services.

- Find out what the setup fee is, as well as any monthly charges. Ask what the lease terms are. The length of the lease determines the pricing. The longer the lease, usually the lower the monthly price. Commonly, 3-, 6-, and 12-month leases are offered.

- Find out the charges for making any changes, and find out how fast the changes are implemented.

- Ask about what kind of traffic the Web site receives on a daily, weekly, or monthly basis. Compare the different figures. These figures will give you a general idea of the pulling power of that site. It also lets you judge the value of the advertising and promotion being conducted by the server service. Traffic can range from just a few thousand hits to several hundred thousand hits a month.

- Get a formal proposal and quote from the server service that includes all costs.

- Find out what the server service charges for any support services required to support a Web server. These costs can be substantial, and they are completely separate from the basic setup and monthly fees. For example, there can be charges for mail forwarding to your e-mail box, HTML authoring, image scanning, editing, format conversion, and other services.

Handling Web Business Transactions

Server services can handle Web transactions in a variety of ways. Many server services retain a percentage of the gross sales of the virtual storefront, much like malls do for their retail tenants. Additionally, server services may charge a host of fees for maintaining and operating your storefront. The storefront lets you choose from a wide variety of customer pricing and the following charge options:

- Item charges, such as a charge per file or document
- Access charges by connection, with no time limits

- Connection-time charges by the amount of time connected

- Subscription charges for individuals, sites, or companies

- Search charges, regardless of success of search

- Hit charges for each successful search result

❏ PROMOTING YOUR WEB PRESENCE

Beyond what the server service does to promote its Web site, you can promote your Web business presence. Chapter 4 explains the general options for promoting your business on the Internet. Specific promotional resources for Web servers are as follows:

- Register your home page with the official list of Web servers at CERN. To do so, point Mosaic to the address *http://info.cern.ch/hypertext/DataSources/WWW/Servers.html* and follow the instructions. In many cases, the server service will do this for you.

- Post an article in the Web newsgroup. Web issues are discussed in the comp.infosystems.www newsgroup. Post an article to this newsgroup only if your server is relevant.

- Subscribe to a Web LISTSERV that provides a forum for general discussion of Web issues by sending e-mail to *listserv@info.cern.ch* with *"add www-announce"* as the body of your message.

- Send an entry to be included to the NCSA What's New page. Send an e-mail message with the attached HTML-formatted document to *whats-new@ncsa.uiuc.edu*. Keep your message concise, and write it in the third person. For example, write "Technology Central announces a new product," not "We announce a new product."

- Register your home page with a free service at M.I.T. List of Commercial Services on the Web. To do so, send an e-mail message to *hhh@mit.edu* with a full description of your Web presence. To view this listing service, point your Web browser to *http://tns-www.lcs.mit.edu:/commerce.html*.

Glossary

□ □ □

Talking the Net Talk

Adobe Acrobat   A technology developed by Adobe Systems that allows documents created on one computer system to be read and printed on other systems, with the fonts, formatting, text attributes, and graphic elements intact. The Adobe Acrobat software family is used to read, view, and print files in Portable Document Format (PDF). The software is divided into three separate packages: The Acrobat Reader (reads PDF files), Acrobat Exchange (reads and saves PDF files), and Acrobat Distiller (converts PostScript files to PDF files).

agent   A broad term used to describe any automated process that performs an action or series of actions with little or no human intervention. Filters and rules used in e-mail programs are types of agents.

alias   A word or number that stands for one or more e-mail addresses. Aliases simplify addressing e-mail messages for groups.

analog line   Voice-grade telecommunications line used for telephones. To communicate with a computer on an analog line requires a modem at each end of the connection—to convert digital information to analog, then back to digital.

anchors   Links added to a Web source document that point to text and images by way of HREFs (hypertext references).

anonymous FTP   A public FTP file archive that any Internet user can access. The term *anonymous* refers to a generic account that is used by anyone to log into an FTP server.

AppleTalk   The built-in network protocol for the Macintosh operating system.

Archie   An Internet tool used for locating files that are publicly accessible at anonymous FTP sites.

articles   Messages posted to USENET newsgroups. Most newsreaders keep messages together to provide a continuous thread of discussion.

ASCII   Universal character set supported by most computer systems. It's the universal text format that can be displayed on any computer on the Internet. ASCII stands for American Standard Code for Information Interchange.

Ask Processing   Allows a Gopher site to present an interactive form or dialog box for the user to fill in to perform any kind of transaction on a Gopher server. This feature is supported in Gopher+, the newest Gopher protocol.

attribute   Assigns keywords for a Gopher item so Internet users can locate it using a keyword search.

AU   Sound file format developed by Sun Microsystems that is recognized by Mosaic Web clients (Microsoft Windows, Macintosh, and X Windows). A separate application is typically used on PCs and Macs to either play back or convert AU files to another format, such as a waveform (WAV) file for Windows.

AUP   Acceptable use policy. A policy established by any network as to what types of activities are allowed on the network. Because the Internet is a network of networks, many AUPs exist. The one most often referred to is the National Science Foundation's AUP. NSF runs the backbone system for the Internet in the United States. This AUP has restricted commercial traffic across the Internet, but like everything on the Internet, it's now changing to include commercial activity.

authentication   A security feature that allows access to information to be granted on an individual basis.

backbone   The high-speed central network that connects and delivers data traffic between regional networks. The backbone system for the U.S. portion of the Internet is NSFNET, which is run by the National Science Foundation.

bandwidth   The range of transmission frequencies that a network can use. The greater the bandwidth, the greater the amount of data that can travel on the network at one time.

B-channels   *See* bearer channels.

bearer channels   The two parts of an ISDN line that can handle up to 64 kbps each for a combined capacity of 128 kbps.

bozo filter   A filter that lets an e-mail user restrict messages from a specified e-mail address.

bps   Bits per second. The speed at which bits are transmitted over a communications medium, such as a telecommunications line or network.

BRI   Basic rate interface. The term used to describe the three channels that make up an ISDN line, including two B-channels (bearer channels) and one D-channel (provides the call-control functions).

BRI terminal adapter   A device used to connect a computer to an ISDN BRI line.

CATV   The term used for the cable system that delivers television. This cable system promises high-speed data communications for Internet connections in the future.

CERN   The Swiss organization that developed the World-Wide Web. The acronym CERN comes from the French Conseil European pour la Récherche Nucleaire (European Laboratory for Particle Physics), which was the previous name for the organization.

class C IP account   A network IP account. A class C IP account includes an IP numeric address that can be used with a router to connect multiple users on a network to the Internet.

classification   An entry for a Gopher site that classifies the type of information available at that site. Classifications are used by Gopher users to narrow a search based on a topic.

client   Any computer remotely connected to a host computer. This term is also used for software used to connect to a host computer, such as a Gopher or Mosaic client program.

client/server computing   The fundamental relationship of computers on the Internet (or any network) where one computer acts as the client to remotely connect to another computer that acts as a server (also called a host).

Common Ground   An application and file format that allows documents with formatted information to be viewed on different platforms. Common Ground documents typically include a viewer program.

compression   The compacting of files to save storage space and reduce the time it takes to transfer files. Various compression formats and programs are available.

content-based marketing   The packaging of your business information as a resource for users on the Internet instead of using traditional advertising copy.

cross-posting The posting of the same article to several newsgroups. Cross-posting of articles with no regard to the newsgroups' areas of interest is called *spamming*.

CSLIP A compressed version of SLIP that allows for faster transfer of information.

CSU/DSU Customer service unit/data service unit. A device that is the equivalent of a digital modem and allows a computer to communicate via digital lines. A CSU/DSU is used only on a dedicated (leased) line connection.

cyberspace A term coined by William Gibson in his book *Neuromancer*. The popularized term refers to the digital world of any network, but it is commonly used to refer to the Internet.

data traffic The amount of information traversing a network. On the Internet, it refers to the number of TCP/IP packets moving through the network. When data traffic for a server you are accessing is heavy, both your system and the server's system slow down.

dedicated port An exclusive port dedicated for a dial-up IP account. A dedicated port ensures access whenever a connection to the service provider is made. Otherwise, if all the service provider's modems are in use, a dial-up IP account will get a busy signal.

dial-up IP account The entry level of Internet Protocol accounts. This low-cost type of account lets computer users dial up a service provider's computer using a modem.

digital line A telecommunications line that transmits data in digital format, which is the way computers handle data. A digital line allows high-speed data transmission. Digital lines are generally leased.

DiskPaper format A file format used to convert Macintosh documents into stand-alone applications that can be viewed and printed without the original application used to generate them.

domain Highest subdivision of the Internet; usually by country or type of organization (educational, commercial, and so on).

domain name The complete domain name address, including the domain and the unique name of the organization, such as *bookware.com*.

DNS Domain name system. The text-based Internet addressing system that connects a domain name to a specified numeric IP address. A domain name is portable, meaning it can remain the same but its IP address can change.

download   Retrieve a file from a server or another computer.

dynamic IP address   A numeric IP address that changes. Using a dynamic IP address means you are assigned a different numeric IP address each time you connect to your service provider.

e-mail   Electronic mail. A network service that enables users to send and receive messages. Communicating via e-mail is the number one use of the Internet.

encryption   The scrambling of a message or file so that it can't be read by anyone except the intended receiver.

error detection   A process used during file transfer to discover discrepancies between transmitted and received data. Some file transfer programs only detect errors, others detect errors and attempt to fix them (called error correction).

Ethernet   A networking standard developed by Xerox with Intel and DEC (Digital Equipment Corporation). Ethernet can connect 1024 workstations and transmit data at a maximum speed of 10 Mbps.

FAQ   Frequently asked questions. A text file that provides information to answer questions that users may have about a particular topic, service, or product.

filter   A program or feature that lets users sort through data. In this book, filters typically refer to e-mail programs used to send mail messages to a particular mail folder.

firewall   The feature that results when some of the packet-sharing network facilities are disabled to protect a network connected to the Internet from being accessed by unauthorized users via the Internet.

flame   An inflammatory remark or message, usually associated with e-mail or an article posted to a network newsgroup.

folders   Special files used for storing e-mail messages.

forwarding   Directing e-mail from one e-mail box to another.

freeware   Software that is free on the net.

FTP   File Transfer Protocol. The medium that allows files to be transferred between computers on the Internet using an FTP program.

FTP program   An application software program that works with the File Transfer Protocol to transfer files between computers.

gateway   Connection point between two e-mail systems or networks that use different protocols. A computer or other device acts as a translator to communicate across different protocols.

GIF   Graphic Interchange Format. A graphics file format that originated on the CompuServe network. Most client programs that include graphics support GIF. For example, GIF is the standard file format for graphics files on the World-Wide Web.

Gopher   This popular protocol lets clients retrieve Internet resources. The Gopher protocol lets you access files and directories across the Internet. A Gopher client can search and retrieve information from hundreds of Gopher servers on the Internet to give the user a seamless view of the distributed information.

Gopher+   An enhanced version of Gopher that includes support for multimedia, forms, and authentication.

Gopherspace   Collectively describes the hundreds of interconnected Gopher servers on the Internet. To a Gopher user, all these Gopher servers form a seamless source of information resources.

GUI   Graphical user interface. A computer interface based on graphical symbols rather than text. The Macintosh operating system and Microsoft Windows are examples of GUIs.

HFS   Hierarchical file structure. The inverted tree structure that most computer systems use for organizing directories and files. The topmost directory of the tree is known as the root directory. All other directories branch out from the root directory.

home page   The first page of a Web site and the starting point for users to navigate the World-Wide Web.

host   A computer that acts as a server to let users remotely access information on that computer.

HREF   *See* hypertext reference.

HTML   Hypertext markup language. The scripting language used to create Web documents. HTML commands specify the layout of a document as it appears on a Web client.

HTML editor   A specialized editor that simplifies creating Web documents using HTML commands. For example, if you are using an HTML editor, HTML commands automatically surround selected text when the user clicks on a button or chooses a menu item.

HTML+ The newest version of the HTML scripting language that includes enhancements over HTML, including image mapping, support for forms, and improved formatting features, such as tables.

HTTD server The most common UNIX server software for the World-Wide Web software developed by NCSA. The server sends the HTML commands to the Web client program to assemble the Web documents at the client computer.

HTTP Hypertext Transport Protocol. The protocol used by the World-Wide Web.

HyperCard An Apple authoring program for creating hypermedia documents called stacks.

hypermedia Another word for multimedia. Hypermedia is frequently used instead of multimedia to imply the inclusion of hypertext in an interactive environment.

hypertext A system of information browsing and retrieval that allows a user to follow linked, non-sequential associative trails of thought instead of a strict linear structure.

INDEX file A text file that lists the files in a directory. Usually included in directories on FTP servers.

Internet The network of networks that connects over 15,000 networks and 38 million people worldwide.

Internet address The combination of the IP numeric address and domain name.

Internet tool Any application used on the Internet that supports one or more protocols. For example, users work with FTP using an FTP client program that uses the File Transfer Protocol to transfer files across the Internet. For every protocol, a tool works with it. Some Internet tools support several protocols. For example, Gopher clients can also access FTP and Telnet sites.

InterNIC Internet Network Information Center. An organization funded by the National Science Foundation to provide information, directory assistance, and domain name registration services.

IP Internet Protocol. The protocol used as a basis of the Internet. The Internet Protocol allows data to travel in packets routed across different networks, then reach their final destination and be reassembled.

ISDN Integrated Services Digital Network. A new generation of digital telecommunications lines being introduced by telephone companies. ISDN lines includes two bearer channels, each of which can handle up to 64 kbps, for a combined capacity of 128 kbps.

JPEG Joint Photographic Experts Group. This group has defined a compression scheme that reduces the size of image files up to 20 times. JPEG-compressed image files typically end with the file name extension .JPG.

kbps Kilobits per second. The data transfer speed on a network, measured in multiples of 1,024 bps.

LAN Local Area Network. A group of computers and other devices that are in close proximity, such as in an office, that are connected together so they can pass data between them.

leased line A telecommunications line, usually digital, that is leased from a service provider or telephone company. Leased lines handle more bandwidth and are charged on a flat monthly rate instead of a measured rate. For businesses connecting several users to the Internet through a LAN or maintaining connections for long periods of time, a leased line is the most economical option.

LISTSERV An e-mail server program for mailing lists.

ls-1R file An index listing of all the files at an FTP site.

mail bombing The bombarding of an e-mail address with messages sent by an angry person or group of people. Mail bombing floods the e-mail account to make it unmanageable. It is not uncommon for mail bombing to overload the mail server.

mailbot An e-mail server that automatically sends out information via e-mail to anyone requesting the information via e-mail.

mailing list A forum where e-mail messages are delivered to the people who subscribe to the list. Some mailing lists are moderated, so people can send messages to the moderator, who in turn decides whether to post the message. A person joins a mailing list by sending a message to a specific e-mail address, which typically is the mail server that sends out the e-mail.

mbps Million bits per second. High speed data transmission rates used primarily by Internet backbones.

MIME Multipurpose Internet Mail Extension. An electronic mail protocol that allows users to attach binary files to e-mail messages. Most mail packages support the MIME protocol.

modem   A piece of equipment that connects a computer to an analog telecommunications line. Modem stands for modulator-demodulator. A modem translates digital data to analog and back again. Modem speeds are measured in bits per second (bps).

Mosaic   The de facto Web client program that was developed by NCSA (National Center for Supercomputing Applications). It is available at no charge for Microsoft Windows, Macintosh, and X Windows platforms. Commercial Web clients are now emerging in growing numbers.

MPEG   Motion Picture Experts Group. A group that created a video file compression format. The MPEG compression format incorporates predictive calculation so the current frame predicts what will be in the following frames. MPEG files usually end with the file extension .MPG.

multitasking operating system   Allows many users to use a computer system to perform many tasks at the same time. UNIX is the most popular multitasking operating system.

National Science Foundation   *See* NSF.

NCSA   National Center for Supercomputing Applications. The organization that developed the Mosaic client for the World-Wide Web.

network news   A UNIX-based (USENET) distributed messaging system with thousands of ongoing discussions, called newsgroups, covering every topic imaginable. People who subscribe to network news communicate using a messaging system similar to e-mail.

newsgroup   A discussion forum in the network news system.

newsreader   A program used to read and post network news. For example, WinVN and Trumpet are two popular Windows newsreaders, and News-Watcher is a popular Macintosh newsreader program.

NFS   Network file system. A protocol designed by Sun Microsystems that allows a computer on a network to use the files and peripherals of another networked computer as if they were local.

NNTP   Network News Transport Protocol. The protocol used to distribute network news.

NSF   National Science Foundation. The U.S. government agency responsible for operation of the Internet backbone for the United States, which is called NSFNET.

NT1   Network Terminator 1. A device, usually an external box, used to split two wires into four to connect a computer to an ISDN line.

packet   A block of data sent over a network. The packet includes the identities of the sending and receiving stations, error-control information, and a message.

packet-switching   The communications technology on which the Internet is based. Packets of digital data are transmitted from many people simultaneously between computers.

PDN   Public Data Network. A telecommunications service that gives access to a nationwide data network through a local phone call.

PDF   Portable document format. The file format for documents created using Adobe Acrobat. PDF documents allow people to share formatted documents across different platforms. To create a PDF document, you use Adobe Acrobat Exchange and print the existing document to a file. The PDF file can be viewed using the Acrobat Reader, which is distributed free.

POP   Post Office Protocol. An e-mail protocol used to retrieve e-mail from a service provider's machine for dial-up accounts. Most people refer to the Post Office Protocol with its version number to avoid confusing it with a point of presence. For example, POP3 refers to Post Office Protocol version 3.

POP   Point of Presence. The closest location or telephone access number for a network or telephone company. Leased-line charges are based in part on how far your location is from a POP.

post   To send a message, called an article, to a network newsgroup.

PostScript   Adobe's proprietary page-description language, designed to relay instructions about fonts and objects to a printer. The de facto standard for the Macintosh, UNIX, and desktop publishing.

POTS   Plain old telephone service. Used to describe standard voice-grade telephone lines. In terms of bandwidth, these lines are at the bottom of the telecommunications hierarchy.

PPP   Point to Point Protocol. A protocol that allows a computer to use the TCP/IP protocols and be directly connected to the Internet using a standard voice telephone line and a high-speed modem. PPP is rapidly replacing SLIP.

Protocol   A specification that describes the rules and procedures so computers can communicate. Most Internet tools are named after the protocols they use. For example, FTP stands for the File Transfer Protocol and is also the name of the program used for transferring files.

publishing   The placing of information on a server to make it available to users on the Internet. The two most popular options for online publishing are Gopher and World-Wide Web.

QuickTime   An Apple technology for real-time video and multiple-media data. QuickTime files can include text, sound, and video, among other formats.

README file   Text file containing important information usually used at FTP sites to describe what is available at that site or other information.

Replica   An application and file format from Farallon that allows documents with formatted information to be viewed on PC and Macintosh platforms. Replica documents include a program for viewing the document.

Router   A hardware device connected to a host on a LAN that acts as a gateway between two different types of networks. For example, a router is used to connect an Ethernet-based network to the TCP/IP-based Internet. Data traffic is routed from individual computers to the router, then through the telecommunications line to the service provider's computer.

RTF   Rich text format. A text file that includes some formatting, such as bold, italic, and underlined text.

rule   A criterion used for filtering or routing incoming e-mail.

serial line   Serial means one by one. A serial line is used to refer to data transmission over a telephone line via a modem or when data goes from a computer to a printer or other device.

server   Computer that can distribute services or resources. A server is often a piece of hardware and software that provides access to information requested from it. A server is also called a host computer.

server service   A business that provides the services and resources required for other businesses to establish a server presence on the Internet. Server services offer an affordable option for businesses that can't afford the cost of establishing their own in-house server.

service provider   An organization that provides connections to the Internet. Some service providers also furnish server services for their customers.

shareware   Software that is available on the net, so you can try it free. If you like the software and want to continue to use it, you send the author a fee to register the product. Shareware is based on the honor system. Registering usually gives you the benefit of technical support and documentation, and in some cases added features are enabled after you register the software.

shell account   A UNIX-based account on a service provider's computer.

signature   A standard sign-off used by people for e-mail and newsgroup posts, often contained in a file and automatically appended to an outgoing mail message or network news post.

SLIP   Serial Line Internet Protocol. A protocol that allows a computer to use the Internet Protocol with a standard voice telephone line and a high-speed modem. SLIP is an older protocol that is being superseded by PPP.

SMTP   Simple Mail Transfer Protocol. The standard Internet protocol for distributing e-mail.

snail mail   Mail delivered by the U.S. Postal Service.

source document   The text-based document that contains the HTML commands for a World-Wide Web document.

spamming   *See* cross-posting.

static IP address   A numeric IP address that does not change each time you connect to a service provider.

subnet address   A number that is used to identify a subnetwork. Using a subnet address (called subnetting) lets different subnetworks on a LAN share the same Internet IP address.

system administrator   The person who manages a network or host computer.

TCP/IP   Transmission Control Protocol and Internet Protocol. The suite of networking protocols that lets disparate types of computers communicate. TCP/IP is the standard protocol upon which the Internet is based.

TCP/IP stack   The software that allows a computer to communicate via TCP/IP.

Telnet   A terminal-emulation protocol that allows Internet users to remotely log onto a host computer using a Telnet program.

throughput   A measure of a network or computer's overall performance that is a function of all the configuration components of a system.

upload   To send a file to a server or another computer.

URL Universal Resource Locator. An addressing scheme used to link resources via the World-Wide Web. All Web clients let you move directly to any supported Internet resource when you enter a URL address.

UNIX A popular multiuser, multitasking operating system developed by AT&T. UNIX served as a foundation for the development of the Internet and continues to be the operating system of choice for most Internet servers. TCP/IP is built into UNIX.

USENET A UNIX-based messaging system that is the basis of network news.

UUCP UNIX-to-UNIX copy. A facility for transferring e-mail and network news in batch form. UUCP is an affordable way for several e-mail accounts to exist under a domain name without using a LAN IP account.

V.32bis Currently the fastest standard modem protocol used by 9600 bps and 14.4 kbps modems. Most V.32bis modems support V.42 error correction and V.42bis data compression.

V.34 The emerging 28.8 kbps standard, scheduled to be ratified by late 1994. While V.34 was under development, some modem manufacturers implemented the unratified standard and called it V.Fast.

Veronica Stands for the Very Easy Rodent-Oriented Net-wide Index to Computerized Archives. Veronica is a useful program for finding specific information in Gopherspace.

viewer programs Specialized programs used to view graphic files online.

virtual commerce The process of conducting business on the Internet using a combination of tools and establishing a server presence for users.

virtual mall A Gopher or World-Wide Web site that lets users visit many businesses online to browse and conduct business. Virtual malls operate on the same concept used by real-world retail malls.

virtual storefront The online version of a full-service storefront, including the publishing of sales materials and the capability of processing credit-card transactions. The two leading types of servers used for establishing a virtual storefront are Gopher and World-Wide Web.

WAIS Wide-area information servers. A powerful system for searching and retrieving information from databases scattered across the Internet.

Waveform Microsoft Windows sound file format. Waveform titles end with the extension .WAV.

Web   Commonly used term for the World-Wide Web.

Webmaster   A system administrator for a World-Wide Web server.

WinSock   A program that conforms to a set of standards called the Windows Socket API. The Windows Socket is a standard for implementing Windows software with a TCP/IP stack. In other words, a WinSock program controls the link between Windows software and a TCP/IP program.

World-Wide Web   A hypermedia-based system for accessing Internet resources. Commonly referred to as the Web, it lets users download files, listen to sounds, view video files, and jump to other documents or Internet sites by using hypertext. The Web also includes gateways to sites using other Internet protocols, such as Gopher and FTP. WWW or W3 are also used to refer to the World-Wide Web.

XBM   X bitmap. A graphics file format for X Windows (UNIX) systems.

X Windows   A graphical environment for the UNIX operating system.

Appendix

❑ ❑ ❑

Internet Business Resources

This resource guide is designed to point you toward specific products and services that we addressed in this book. Keep in mind that new services and products for businesses are coming online rapidly, so this is by no means a complete listing.

❑ CONNECTION SOFTWARE

There is a growing variety of software for connecting PCs and Macintoshes to the Internet. These software packages let PCs and Macintoshes speak TCP/IP, which is the language of the Internet. Other connection software options include UUCP programs for e-mail and network news, and standard communications programs that have added Internet applications to their suite of tools. The following sections describe these software options.

TCP/IP for PCs (DOS/Windows)

TCP/IP products change fast, so no listing can be complete. Throughout this project, we used Chameleon from NetManage. Be aware that a growing number of service providers are offering TCP/IP software as a part of the account. For example, NETCOM offers a TCP/IP program called NetCruiser with an IP account. Other service providers are offering a similar TCP/IP program called Pipeline as part of establishing an IP account. Before purchasing a TCP/IP package, ask your service provider if it bundles a TCP/IP package with IP accounts.

Information Sources

Information on TCP/IP and NFS (network file system) software is available at the following World-Wide Web URLs:

http://www.rtd.com/pcnfsfaq/faq.html

hhtp://www.cis.ohio-state.edu/hypertext/faq/usenet/ibmpc-tcp-ip/faq.html

You can also get information on TCP/IP from the following network news-groups:

comp.protocols.tcp-ip.ibmpc

comp.protocols.nfs

alt.winsock

comp.sys.ibm.pc.hardware.networking

The following FTP sites contain up-to-date information on TCP/IP software:

Site: ftp.rtd.com
Directory: pub/tcpip/pcnfsfaq.zip

Site: ftp.netcom.com
Directory: /pub/mailcom/IBMTCP/ibmtcp.zip

Site: sunsite.unc.edu
Directory: micro/pc-stuff/ms-windows/winsock

Products

AIR NFS
AIR
AIR CORE
AIR SQL
AIR X

Spry, Inc.
316 Occidental Avenue South, Suite 200
Seattle, WA 98104
Voice: (800) 777-9638 or (206) 447-0300
Fax: (206) 447-9008
E-mail: info@spry.com
URL: http://www.spry.com

BW-Connect TCP for DOS and Windows
BW-Connect NFS for Microsoft 3.1
BW-Connect NFS for LAN Workplace 3.1
BW-Connect NFS for Windows NT 3.1

Beame & Whiteside, Ltd.
606 Hillsborough Street
Raleigh, NC 27603-1655
Voice: (800) 463-6637 or (919) 831-8989
Fax: (919) 831-8990
E-mail: sales@bws.com

Chameleon v4.0
Chameleon NFS v4.0
Chameleon 32 v4.0 (NT)
Chameleon 32 NFS v4.0
Chameleon X v4.0
Chameleon NFS/X v4.0
Chameleon D (DOS) v4.0
Chameleon NFS/D (DOS) v4.0
Internet Chameleon

NetManage, Inc.
10725 North De Anza Boulevard
Cupertino, CA 95014
Voice: (408) 973-7171
Fax: (408) 257-6405
E-mail: info@netmanage.com

Distinct TCP/IP Tools

Distinct Corporation
12901 Saratoga Avenue
P.O. Box 3410
Saratoga, CA 95070
Voice: (408) 366-8933
Fax: (408) 366-0153
E-mail: mktg@distinct.com

Intercon TCP/Connect II

InterCon Systems Corporation
950 Herndon Parkway, Suite 420
Herndon, VA 22070
Voice: (703) 709-9890
Fax: (703) 709-5555
E-mail: comment@intercon.com

Internet in a Box

Spry, Inc.
316 Occidental Avenue South, Suite 200
Seattle, WA 98104
Voice: (800) 777-9638 or (206) 447-0300
Fax: (206) 447-9008
E-mail: info@spry.com

O'Reilly and Associates, Inc.
103 Morris Street, Suite A
Sebastopol, CA 95472
Voice: (800) 777-9638
E-mail: info@ibox.com
URL: http://www.gnn.com

LAN Workgroup v4.12
LAN WorkPlace for DOS v4.12
LAN WorkPlace for Mac v1.3

Novell Inc.
2180 Fortune Drive
San Jose, CA 95131
Voice: (801) 429-7000 or (800) 243-8526
E-mail: info@novell.com
URL: http://www.novell.com

PathWay Access on DOS/Windows v3.0
PathWay Access Macintosh v2.1

The Wollongong Group Inc.
1129 San Antonio Road
P.O. Box 51860
Palo Alto, CA 94303

Voice: (800) 872-8649 (Outside CA) or (800) 962-8649 (CA) or (415) 962-7100
Fax: (415) 962-0286
E-mail: sales@twg.com

PC-NFS v5.1

SunSoft
Two Elizabeth Drive
Chelmsford, MA 01824
Voice: (508) 442-2300
Fax: (508) 250-2300
URL: http://www.sun.com

PC/TCP OnNet for DOS/Windows v1.1

FTP Software, Inc.
100 Brickstone Square
North Andover, MA 01810
Voice: (800) 282-4387 or (508) 685-4000
Fax: (508) 794-4477
E-mail: info@ftp.com

Piper/IP
Acadia/VxD

Ipswitch, Inc.
333 North Avenue
Wakefield, MA 01880
Voice: (617) 246-1150
Fax: (617) 245-2975
E-mail: info@ipswitch.com

SuperTCP v4.0
SuperTCP NFS v4.0

Frontier Technologies
10201 North Port Washington Road
Mequon, WI 53092
Voice: (414) 241-4555
Fax: (414) 241-7084
E-mail: tcp@frontiertech.com

Trumpet Winsock (Shareware)

Author: Peter R. Tattam (University of Tasmania)
E-mail: peter@psychnet.psychol.utas.edu.au
Site: ftp.utas.edu.au
Directory: /pc/trumpet/

TCP/IP and PPP/SLIP Software for the Macintosh

MacTCP is the standard TCP/IP stack for the Macintosh. It's bundled with most Macintosh connection products, but it can also be purchased separately. Several packages let you add PPP and SLIP support to MacTCP. We used VersaTerm with VersaTilities from Synergy Software, InterCon's TCP Connect II Extended Version, and the InterSLIP program on our Power Macintosh throughout this project.

Products

InterPPP for Macintosh v1.0

InterCon Systems Corporation
950 Herndon Parkway, Suite 420
Herndon, VA 22070
Voice: (703) 709-9890
Fax: (703) 709-5555
E-mail: comment@intercon.com

InterSLIP (Free)

Author: InterCon
Site: ftp.intercon.com
Directory: /intercon/sales

InterCon Systems Corporation
950 Herndon Parkway, Suite 420
Herndon, VA 22070
Voice: (703) 709-9890
Fax: (703) 709-5555
E-mail: comment@intercon.com

MacPPP vl.13 (Free)

Author: Larry Blunk
Site: merit.edu
Directory: /pub/ppp/mac

MacSLIP

TriSoft
1825 East 38½ Street
Austin, TX 78722
Voice: (512) 472-0744
Fax: (512) 473-2122

MacTCP v2.0.x

APDA (Apple Programmers and Developers Association)
P.O. Box 319
Buffalo, NY 14207
Voice: (800) 282-2732 or (800) 767-2775 (Tech support)
Fax: (716) 871-6511
E-mail: apda@applink.apple.com

TCP/Connect II v1.2
Basic version
Extended version
Tools & Toys

InterCon Systems Corporation
950 Herndon Parkway, Suite 420
Herndon, VA 22070
Voice: (703) 709-9890
Fax: (703) 709-5555
E-mail: comment@intercon.com

VersaTerm with VersaTilities v5.0
VersaTerm-PRO v5.0
VersaTilities 1.1

Synergy Software
2457 Perkiomen Avenue
Reading, PA 19606
Voice: (215) 779-0522 or (800) 876-8376

Fax: (215) 370-0548
E-mail: maxwell@sales.synergy.com

UUCP

UUCP offers an affordable option for establishing several e-mail boxes without setting up a LAN IP account. UUCP software allows your business to retrieve its e-mail from the service provider's computer. Once you retrieve the e-mail, you can route it on your local network. UUCP software also lets you download and distribute network news. The best UUCP package for Windows is MKS Internet Anywhere. On the Macintosh side, we recommend UUCP/Connect from InterCon.

Products

MKS Internet Anywhere

MKS
35 King Street North
Waterloo, Ontario
Canada N2N 2W9
Voice: or (800) 265-2797 or (519) 884-2251
Fax: (519) 884-8861
E-mail: inquiry@mks.com

RamNet/UUCP 1.4 (Windows)

Software Concepts Design
P.O. Box 355
New Kingston, NY 12459
Voice: (914) 586-2023
Fax: (914) 586-2025
E-mail: ramnet@ramnet.com

UUCP/Connect Server
UUCP/Connect Client

InterCon Systems Corporation
950 Herndon Parkway, Suite 420
Herndon, VA 22070
Voice: (703) 709-9890
Fax: (703) 709-5555
E-mail: comment@intercon.com

UULINK

Vortex Technology
23241 Ventura Boulevard, Suite 208
Woodland Hills, CA 91364
Voice: (818) 225-2800
Fax: (818) 225-7203
E-mail: sales@vortex.com

UUPC v3.0 (Free)

Author: David Platt
Site: sumex-aim.stanford.edu
Directory: /infomac/comm
E-mail: dplatt@snulbug.mtview.ca.us.

UUPlus

UUPlus
P.O. Box 8
Camarillo, CA 93011
Voice: (805) 485-0057
E-mail: info@uuplus.com

Waffle (Shareware)

Author: Thomas E. Dell
Site: zeus.ieee.org
Directory: /fidonet/ufgate

Thomas E. Dell
P.O. Box 4436
Mountain View, CA 94040
E-mail: dell@vox.darkside.com

Communications Software with Internet Tools

Communications software is currently a small category, but more will probably be available. In fact, only one program fits this catagory: Microphone Pro. This exceptional communications package includes MacTCP, MacSLIP, and several Internet tools, such as Internet Mail, Internet News, Fetch, and TurboGopher. Any Mac user can get connected to the Internet with an IP account and this package.

Products

Microphone Pro 2.0

Software Ventures Corporation
2907 Claremont Avenue
Berkeley, CA 94705
Voice: (510) 644-3232
Fax: (510) 848-0885
E-mail: microphone@svcdudes.com

☐ CONNECTION HARDWARE

On the hardware side of getting your business wired to the Internet are three hardware product categories: modems, routers, and ISDN adapters. Modems are for single dial-up IP accounts, routers are for connecting small LANs to the Internet, and an ISDN adapter is for connecting a computer to the next generation of telecommunications line, ISDN.

Modems

For a dial-up IP account, the most important thing you can do for yourself is to purchase a fast modem. It is a good idea to find out what modem speeds your service provider supports to make sure you are getting all the speed you can. Throughout this project, we used the US Robotics Courier and Intel 144/144E modems on our PCs, we used the Teleport Mercury from Global Village on our Power Mac. You should be aware that some modem manufacturers, such as US Robotics and Hayes, are offering upgrades to the V.34 (V.Fast) standard when the standard is finalized. The V.34 modems can handle data speeds of 28.8 kbps.

Products

TelePort/Mercury
Global Village Communication
685 East Middlefield Road Bldg. B
Mountain View, CA 94043
Voice: (415) 390-8200
Fax: (415) 390-8282
E-mail: techsupport@globalvillag.com

Accura 288 V.FC +FAX
Hayes Optima 288 V.FC +FAX
Hayes Optima 288B V.FC +FAX Internal (includes the ESP
  Communications Accelerator)
Hayes Optima 288 V.FC +FAX for the Macintosh
ESP Communications Accelerator Version 2, Single port or Dual port
(serial accelerator card)

Hayes Microcomputer Products, Inc.
P.O. Box 105203
Atlanta, GA 30348
Voice: (404) 441-1617
Fax: (404) 441-1213
Faxback: (800) 429-3739
BBS: (800) 874-2937 or (404) 446-6336

PM14400FXSA V.32bis
PM14400FXMT V.32bis

Practical Peripherals
31245 La Baya Drive
Westlake Village, CA 91362
Voice: (800) 442-4774 or (818) 706-0333
Fax: (818) 706-2474

FastBlazer
Telebit WorldBlazer
Telebit T3000
QBlazer Plus (Portable Modem)

Telebit
1315 Chesapeake Terrace
Sunnyvale, CA 94089
Voice: (800) 835-3248 or (408) 734-4333
Fax: (408) 734-3333
E-mail: info@telebit.com

Intel SatisFAXtion 400
Intel SatisFAXtion 400e

Intel 144/144e
Intel 144/144 Internal

Intel Corporation
Personal Computer Enhancement Division
5200 NE Elam Young Parkway
Hillsboro, OR 97124-6497
Voice: (800) 538-3373 or (503) 696-8080
Fax: (503) 629-7576
Faxback: (800) 525-3019
BBS: (503) 645-6275

US Robotics Courier Dual Standard
US Robotics Courier HST
US Robotics Sportster 28,200 Data/Fax with V.FC
US Robotics Sportster 28,200 Data/Fax with V.FC internal
US Robotics Sportster 28,200 Mac&Fax with V.FC
WorldPort 2496
LAN modem with Dial Routing

U.S. Robotics
8100 North McCormick Boulevard
Skokie, IL 60076-2999
Voice: (800) 342-5877 or (708) 982-5010
Fax: (708) 982-5235
BBS: (708) 982-5092
E-mail: sales@usr.com

ZyXEL U-1496 plus
ZyXEL U-1496E plus
ZyXEL U-1496E
ZyXEL U-1496B
ZyXEL U-1496B plus
ZyXEL U-1496P Portable

ZYXEL USA
4920 East LaPalma Avenue
Anaheim, CA 92807
Voice: (714) 693-0808
Fax: (714) 693-0705
BBS:(714) 693-0762
E-mail: sales@zyxel.com

Routers

Routers offer the best low-cost solutions for small businesses that want to connect their PC or Macintosh network to the Internet using a LAN IP account. As the small-business Internet-connection market heats up, a growing number of new routers at lower prices are becoming available. Many router companies make deals with service providers to bundle their products with accounts. Before purchasing a router, make sure your service provider guarantees it can work with the router. Some service providers support only certain routers. Typically, you can get a price break on a router by purchasing it from a service provider as part of an Internet account.

Products

Access Node Routers
1 Ethernet and 2 Synchronous
1 Token Ring and 2 Synchronous
1 Ethernet, 1 Token Ring, and 2 Synchronous
1 Ethernet, 1 Synchronous, and 1 ISDN BRI
1 Token Ring, 1 Synchronous, and 1 ISDN BRI

Wellfleet Communications
8 Federal Street
Billerica, MA 01821
Voice: (508) 670-8888
Fax: (508) 436-3658

Cisco 2501 (Ethernet)
Cisco 2502 (Token Ring)
Cisco 2503 (Ethernet Serial and ISDN BRI)
Cisco 2504 (Token Ring with ISDN BRI)
Cisco 508-CS (Communications Server), 8 ports
Cisco 516-CS (Communications Server), 16 ports
Cisco 4000

Cisco Systems, Inc.
170 West Tasman
San Jose, CA 95134
Voice: (800) 553-6387 or (408) 526-4000
Fax: (408) 526-4100

Morning Star PPP
Morning Star Express 2E Router
Morning Star Express PC Router Kit
Morning Star SnapLink

Morning Star Technologies
1760 Zollinger Road
Columbus, OH 43221-2856
Voice: (800) 558-7827
Fax: (614) 459-5054
E-mail: sales@morningstar.com.
URL: www.morningstar.com

NetBlazer PN-1 (2 dial-up ports with modem)
NetBlazer PN-2 (2 dial-up ports, no modem)
NetBlazer PN-4 (4 dial-up ports, no modem)

Telebit
1315 Chesapeake Terrace
Sunnyvale, CA 94089
Voice: (800) 835-3248 or (408) 734-4333
Fax: (408) 734-3333
E-mail: info@telebit.com

NetHopper
NH-P (1 Ethernet, 1 modem port)
NH-3 (3 modems, 1 Ethernet port)
NH-5 (5 modems, 1 Ethernet port)
NH-SYNCH+ (1 modem, 1 Ethernet, 1 synchronous port)
NHRC (Remote Client Software)

Rockwell International Corporation
7402 Hollister Avenue
Santa Barbara, CA 93117-2590
Voice: (800) 262-8023 or (805) 968-4262
Fax: (805) 968-6478
E-mail: info@rns.com or sales@rns.com
URL: http://www.rns.com

Pipeline MAX
Pipeline 400
Pipeline 100

Ascend Communications, Inc.
1275 Harbor Parkway
Alameda, CA 94502
Voice: (510) 769-6001
Fax: (510) 814-2300
E-mail: info@ascend.com

Portmaster-2 (10 serial, 1 parallel, 1 Ethernet port)
Portmaster-2E-10 (10 serial, 1 parallel, 1 Ethernet port)
Portmaster-2E-20 (20 serial, 1 parallel, 1 Ethernet port)
Portmaster-2E-30 (30 serial, 1 parallel, 1 Ethernet port)

Livingston Enterprises, Inc.
6920 Koll Center Parkway, Suite 220
Pleasanton, CA 94566
Voice: (800) 458-9966 or (510) 426-0770
Fax: (510) 426-8951
E-mail: sales@livingston.com

ISDN Hardware

As ISDN service opens up, a flood of companies will offer ISDN products. Most phone companies work with local distributers to provide ISDN equipment. Check with your local phone company for ISDN equipment resellers in your area. The following list of ISDN-specific hardware allows computers to connect with an ISDN line.

Products

Everywhere 160
Everywhere 200
Everywhere 300
Everywhere 900

Combinet
333 West El Camino Real
Sunnyvale, CA 94087
Voice: (408) 522-9020

Fax: (408) 732-5479
E-mail: info@combinet.com sales@combinet.com

Hayes ISDN Terminal Adapter

Hayes Microcomputer Products, Inc.
P.O. Box 105203
Atlanta, GA 30348
Voice: (404) 441-1617
Fax: (404) 441-1213
Faxback: (800) 429-3739
BBS: (800) 874-2937

IBM WaveRunner Digital Modem

IBM Direct
4111 Northside Parkway
Atlanta, GA 30327
Voice: (800) 426-2255
Faxback: (800) 426-4329

IMAC (One ISDN Connection)
Dual IMAC (Two ISDN Connections)
PC IMA-ISA (ISDN ISA network interface card for PC servers)
PC IMAC-MC (ISDN Micro Channel network interface card for PC servers)
PC IMAC/4-X (Multiport ISDN network card)
PC IMAC for NetWare Systems

Digiboard Electronics
6400 Flying Cloud Drive
Eden Prarie, MN 55344
Voice: (800) 344-4273
Fax: (612) 943-5398
E-mail: info@digibd.com
URL: hhtp://www.digibd.com

ISU 128 (Terminal Adaptor, NT1, and power supply)
NT1 (Standalone)
NT1PS (Power Supply)
NT1 Integrated (includes internal power supply)

ADTRAN
901 Explorer Blvd.
Huntsville, AL 35806-2807
Voice: (800) 827-0807 or (205) 971-8000
Fax: (205) 971-8699

NT1U-220TC (NT1)
901034 (Power Supply)

Tone Commander Systems
4370 150th N.E.
Redmond, Washington 98073-9739
Voice: (800) 524-0024
Fax: (206) 881-7179
E-mail: info@connected.com

Pipeline 50 ISDN Router

Ascend Communications, Inc.
1275 Harbor Bay Parkway
Alameda, CA 94502
Voice: (510) 769-6001
Fax: (510) 814-2300
E-mail: info@ascend.com

❏ CONSULTANTS

Many consultants offer services for establishing a business presence on the Internet, with specialties ranging from networking to Internet marketing. The following consultants are the ones we know about.

Services

Applied Network Communications Inc.
20 South Santa Cruz Avenue, Suite 303
Los Gatos, CA 95030

Voice: (408) 395-7374
Fax: (408) 399-4556
E-mail: scotts@netcom.com

Core Competence, Inc.
David M. Piscitello
1620 Tuckerstown Road
Dresher, PA 19025
E-mail: dave@corecom.com

Cyberspace Development, Inc.
3700 Cloverleaf Drive
Boulder, CO 80304
Voice: (303) 938-8684
Fax: (303) 546-9667
E-mail: office@marketplace.com
URL: http://marketplace.com

David Strom, Inc.
938 Port Washington Boulevard
Port Washington, NY 11050
Voice: (516) 944-3407
E-mail: david@strom.com

Genesis Information Systems
6866 Weller Street
San Diego, CA 92122
Voice: (619) 587-8911
Fax: (619) 546-3919
E-mail: mcculley@netcom.com

Great Circle Associates
1057 West Dana Street
Mountain View, CA 94041
Voice: (415) 962-0841
Fax: (415) 962-0842
E-mail: info@greatcircle.com

Internet Works, Inc.
9988 Whitewater Drive
Burke, VA 20015
Voice: (703) 978-9122
Fax: (703) 978-7147
E-mail: hwylen@access.digex.net

Intuitive Systems
P.O. Box 2781
West Lafayette, IN 47906
Voice: (317) 497-2400
E-mail: taylor@netcom.com

John Mayes & Associates
P.O. Box 1202
Redwood City, CA 94064
Voice: (415) 364-1127
Fax: (415) 364-3035
E-mail: jcm@jma.com

Lloyd Internetworking
3032 Alhambra Drive, Suite 102
Cameron Park, CA 95682
Voice: (916) 676-1147
Fax: (916) 676-3442
E-mail: info@lloyd.com

NetPartners
4010 Park Newport, Suite 217
Newport Beach, CA 92660
Voice: (714) 759-1641
Fax: (714) 644-0577
E-mail: info@netpart.com

The Internet Group
245 Lehigh Avenue
Pittsburgh, PA 15232
Voice: (412) 661-4247
Fax: (412) 661-6927
E-mail: info@tig.com

❏ INTERNET TOOLS SOFTWARE

Beyond TCP/IP connection software are a growing number of specialized
tools for Windows and Macintosh platforms, including e-mail, FTP, newsreaders, Gopher, and World-Wide Web. In most cases, these specialized programs are better than the ones bundled with TCP/IP programs.

E-mail Programs

You can choose from a variety of solutions other than bundled mail programs for getting mail. Along with Chameleon's mail program, we used the Eudora Mail program from Qualcomm throughout this project.

Products

BeyondMail vl.l

Beyond, Inc.
17 New England Executive Park
Burlington, MA 01803
Voice: (508) 898-1000
Fax: (617) 229-1114

Eudora for the Macintosh vl.3 (Free)

Site: ftp sumex-aim.stanford-edu
Directory: /infomac/conan
or
Site: ftp.qualcomm.com
Directory: /mac/eudora

Eudora for Windows vl.0 (Free)

Site: ftp.qualcomm.com
Directory: /pc/eudora

Eudora for the Macintosh v2.0 (Commercial Macintosh Version)
Eudora for Windows v2.0 (Commercial Windows Version)

QUALCOMM
10555 Sorrento Valley Road
San Diego, CA 92121-1617
Voice: (619) 597-5103
Fax: (619) 587-8276
email: jwn2@qualcomm.com

Lotus CC:Mail
Lotus CC: Mail
Lotus Link to SMTP

Lotus Development Corporation
55 Cambridge Parkway
Cambridge, MA 02142
Voice: (800) 343-5414 or (617) 577-8500
Fax: (617) 693-3899

Pronto

CommTouch Software, Inc.
1206 West Hillsdale Boulevard, Suite C
San Mateo, CA 94403
Voice: (800) 777-6686 or (415) 578-6580
Fax: (415) 578-8580
E-mail: pronto@commtouch.com

QuickMail v2.6

CE Software
1801 Industrial Circle
P.O. Box 65580
West Des Moines, IA 50265
Voice: (800) 523-7638
Fax: (515) 221-1806
E-mail: sales%cedsm@uunet.uu.net

SelectMAIL for Windows

SunSelect
Two Elizabeth Drive
Chelmsford, MA 01824
Voice: (508) 442-2300
Fax: (508) 250-2300
URL: http://www.sun.com

WordPerfect Office (Windows)
WordPerfect Office (DOS)

WordPerfect Office (Macintosh)
WordPerfect Office SMTP Gateway

WordPerfect Corporation
1555 N. Technology Way
Orem, Utah 84057-2399
Voice: (800) 451-5151
Fax: (801) 222-5077

FTP

Several FTP packages are available. We used Netmanage's FTP tool throughout this project, but a similar stand-alone FTP tool for Windows is WinFTP.
On the Macintosh side, Fetch is the de facto standard.

Products

Fetch v2.1 (Free for Nonprofits/Macintosh)

Author: Jim Matthews (Dartmouth)
Site: sumex-aim.stanford.edu
Directory: /info-mac/comm

Fetch 2.1 (Commercial/Macintosh)

Software Sales
Dartmouth College
6028 Kiewit Computation Center
Hanover, NH 03755-3523
E-mail: fetch@dartmouth.edu

FTPD v2.1 (Shareware)

Author: Peter Lewis
10 Earlston Way
Booragoon, Perth
WA 6154, Australia
E-mail: peter@cujo.curtin.ed.au
Site: sumex-aim.stanford.edu
Directory: /info-mac/comm

WinFTP (Free/Windows)

Author: Santanu Lahiri
E-mail: slahiri@magnus.acs.ohio-state.edu
Site: ftp.cica.indiana.edu
Directory: /pub/pc/win3/winsock

WS FTP (Free/Windows)

Author: John Junod
Site: ftp.cica.indiana.edu
Directory: /pub/pc/win3/winsock

Newsreaders

Most TCP/IP and UUCP packages come with newsreader programs that let you work with network news. Many of the bundled newsreaders don't offer the features of stand-alone newsreaders. The following are a few popular newsreader programs. WinVN and Trumpet are both popular network news-readers for Windows.

Products

NewsWatcher (Free/Macintosh)

Author: John Norstad
E-mail: j-norstad@nwu.edu
Site: ftp.acns.nwu.edu
Directory: pub/newswatcher

Trumpet (Free/Windows)

Author: Peter R. Tattam (University of Tasmania)
E-mail: peter@psychnet.psychol.utas.edu.au
Site: ftp.utas.edu.au
Directory: /pc/trumpet/

WinVN (Free/Windows)

Author: Mark Riordan
Site: ftp.ksc.nasa.gov
Directory: /pub/win3/winvn

Gopher

Because of Gopher's continued popularity, Gopher clients are popping up everywhere. The two Windows Gopher clients that we used throughout this project were WinGopher and WSGopher. On the Macintosh, TurboGopher is our favorite client.

Products

GopherBook (Free/Windows)

Author: Kevin Gamiel
E-mail: kevin_gamiel@unc.edu
Site: sunsite.unc.edu
Directory: /pub/micro/pc-stuff/ms-windows/winsock/apps

HGopher vl.0 Winsock Version (Free/Windows)
HnGopher v1.0 PC-NFS Version (Free/Windows)

Site: lister.cc.ic.ac.uk
Directory: /pub/wingopher
or
Site: bunsite.unc.edu
Directory: /pub/micro/pc-stuff/ms-windows/winsock/apps/

TurboGopher vl.3 (Free/Macintosh)

Author: University of Minnesota
Site: sumex-aim.stanford.edu
Directory: /info-mac/conun
E-mail: gopher@boombox.micro.umn.edu

WinGopher (Commercial)
WinGopher Complete—Includes TCP/IP stack (Commercial)

Notis Systems Inc.
1007 Church Street
Evanston, IL 60201-3665
Voice: (800) 556-6847 or (708) 866-0150
Fax: (708) 866-4970
E-mail:wingopher@notis.com

WSGopher (Free/Windows)

Author: EG&G of Idaho, Inc.
Site: boombox.micro.unm.edu
Directory: /pub/gopher

World-Wide Web

Mosaic, developed by NCSA and available for free, is the leading World-Wide Web browser for Microsoft Windows, Macintosh, and X Windows platforms. With the explosive popularity of the Web, a growing number of commercial Web browsers are becoming available. We used the Windows version of Mosaic throughout this project. NCSA's Mosaic for Windows is a 32-bit application. NCSA also includes a Windows and Windows for Workgroups 32-bit upgrade, which is also available from Microsoft. On the Macintosh side, we give MacWeb from EINet two thumbs up.

Products

NCSA Mosaic for Macintosh (Free)

Author: Mosaic for Mac Development Team
E-mail: mosaic-mac@ncsa.uiuc.edu
Site: ftp.ncsa.uiuc.edu
Directory: /Mac/Mosaic

NCSA Mosaic for Windows (Free)

Author: Chris Wilson and John Mittelhauser
E-mail: mosaic-win@ncsa.uiuc.edu
Site: ftp.ncsa.uiuc.edu
Directory: /PC/Mosaic

NCSA

National Center for Supercomputing Applications
University of Illinois
152 CAB
605 East Springfield
Champaign, IL 61820
URL: http://www.ncsa.edu

MacWeb (Free)

Site: ftp.einet.net
Directory: /einet/mac/macweb

EINet
Enterprise Integration Network
Microelectronics and Computer Technology Corporation
3500 West Balcones Center Drive
Austin, TX 78759-5398
Voice: (512) 343-0978
Fax: (512) 338-3600
E-mail: macweb@einet.net
URL: http://galaxy.einet.net

MacWWW vl.02 (Free)

Site: cern.ch
Directory: /pub/www/bin/mac

Cello (Free/Windows)

Author: Thomas R. Bruce
Site: fatty.law.cornell.edu
Directory: /pub/LII/Cello

HTML Editors

HTML editors simplify creating Web documents. Currently, only a few HTML editors are available for the PC and Macintosh. More HTML editors are imminent, however.

Products

BBEdit LITE Macintosh (Free)
BBEdit Macintosh (Commercial)

Bare Bones Software
1 Larkspur Way, Suite 4
Natick, MA 01760
Voice: (508) 651-3561
Fax: (508) 651-7584
E-mail: bbedit@world.std.com

HTML HyperEdit for Windows (Free)

Author: Steve Hancock
E-mail: s.hancock@info.curtin.edu.au
Site: info.curtin.edu.au
Directory: /pub/internet/mswindows/hyperedit

Portable Document Software (PDS)

Portable document software lets people share documents with users on different platforms. Our favorite program for sharing documents is Adobe's Acrobat. Now that Adobe has opened up the architecture for Acrobat and is providing the Reader program for free, it's likely that Acrobat will become an Internet standard.

Products

Adobe Acrobat Reader (Free)
Adobe Acrobat Exchange
Adobe Acrobat Network Distiller
Adobe Acrobat Personal Distiller
Adobe Acrobat Starter Kit (Multiplatform, 10 sets)

Adobe Systems Incorporated
1585 Charleston Road
P.O. Box 7900
Mountain View, CA 94039-7900
Voice: (800) 862-3623 or (800) 833-6687
Fax: (415) 961-3769

Common Ground

No Hands Software Inc.
1301 Shoreway Road
Belmont, CA 94002
Voice: (415) 802-5800
Fax: (415) 593-6868
E-mail: nohands@netcom.com

Replica for Windows
Replica for Macintosh

Farallon Computing, Inc.
2470 Mariner Square Loop
Alameda, CA 94501-1010
Voice: (510) 814-5000
Fax: (510) 814-5023
E-mail: cs@farallon.com or farallon@farallon.com
URL: http://www.farallon.com

❑ SERVER SERVICES

Server services are springing up everywhere. Each one offers different kinds of server services, and each has its own pricing scheme. Our best advice is to shop around. In addition to independent server services, a growing number of service providers are also offering server services. Note that some of the companies listed here are also listed as service providers.

Services

Bedrock Solutions
8000 Towers Crescent Drive, Suite 1350
Vienna, VA 22182
Voice: (703) 760-7898
Fax: (703) 760-7899
E-mail: info@bedrock.com
URL: http://end2.bedrock.com

Branch Infomation Services
2607 Patricia
Ann Arbor, MI 48103
Voice: (313) 995-8783
Fax: (313) 995-1931
E-mail: jon@branch.com
URL: http://branch.com

Clark Internet Services, Inc.
10600 Route 108
Ellicott City, MD 21042
Voice: (800) 735-2258

Fax: (410) 730-9765
E-mail: info@clarknet
URL: http://www.clark.net

CommerceNet
450 Hamilton Avenue
Palo Alto, CA 94301
Voice: (415) 617-8790
Fax: (415) 617-8019

CTS Network Services
4444 Convoy Street, Suite 300
San Diego, CA 92111
Voice: (619) 637-3637
Fax: (619) 637-3639
Data: (619) 637-3630 log in as help
E-mail: support@cts.com
URL: http://www.cts.com

Cyberspace Development, Inc.
3700 Cloverleaf Drive
Boulder, CO 80304
Voice: (303) 938-8684
Fax: (303) 546-9667
E-mail: office@marketplace.com
URL: http://marketplace.com

Electric Press, Inc.
11440 Isaac Newton Square
Reston, VA 22090
Voice: (703) 742-3308
Fax: (703) 742-4648
E-mail: info@elpress.com
URL: http://www.elpress.com

Global City
Kaleidospace
P.O. Box 341556
Los Angeles, CA 90034
Voice: (310) 399-4349
Fax: (310) 396-5489

Global Electronic Marketing Service
200 Elmwood Davis Road, Suite 102
Liverpool, NY 13088
Voice: (315) 453-2035

Global Network Navigator (GNN)
103A Morris Street
Sebastopol, CA 95472
Voice: (800) 998-9938
Fax: (707) 829-0104
E-mail: intro.gnn.com
URL: http://www.gnn.com

Internet Ad Emporium
Multimedia Ink Designs
Voice: (619) 679-8317
E-mail: rdegel@ctsnet.cts.com
URL: http://mmink.cts.com/mmink/mmi.html

The Internet Company
96 Sherman Street
Cambridge, MA 02140
Voice: (617) 547-4731
Fax: (617) 547-9064
E-mail: info@internet.com
URL: http://www.internet.com

Internet Distribution Services, Inc.
665 Wellsbury Way
Palo Alto, CA 94306
Voice: (415) 856-8265
Fax: (415) 856-8165
E-mail: marcf@netcom.com
URL: http://www.service.com

Internet Marketing, Inc.
2162 NW Everett, Office #2
Portland, OR 97210
Voice: (503) 226-9128
Fax: (503) 224-1749
E-mail: advertiz@mcs.com

Internet Media Services
644 Emerson Street, Suite 21
Palo Alto, CA 94301
Voice: (415) 328-4638
Fax: (415) 328-4350
E-mail: info@netmedia.com
URL: http://netmedia.com

Internet Shopping Network
P.O. Box 2187
Menlo Park, CA 94026
Voice: (415) 462-1248
Fax: (415) 321-9309

The Internet StoreFront
XOR Network Engineering
Voice: (303) 440-6093
E-mail: info@xor.com

InterNex Information Services, Inc.
1050 Chestnut Street, Suite 202
Menlo Park, CA 94025
Voice: (415) 473-3060
Fax: (415) 473-3062
E-mail: info@internex.net
URL: http://www.internex.net

The Little Garden (TLG)
P.O. Box 410923
San Francisco, CA 94141
Voice: (415) 487-1902
E-mail: info@tlg.org
URL: http://tig.org

MecklerWeb
11 Ferry Lane West
Westport, CT 06880
Voice: (203) 226-6967
Fax: (203) 454-5840
E-mail: mweb@mecklermedia.com

Metasystems Design Group, Inc.
2000 North 15th Street, Suite 103
Arlington, VA 22201
Voice: (703) 243-6622
Fax: (703) 841-9798
E-mail: info@tmn.com
URL: http://www.tmn.com

NetMarket
329 Main Dunstable Road
Nashua, NH 03062
Voice: (603) 881-3777
Fax: (603) 881-3776
E-mail: staff@netmarket.com
URL: http://www.netmarket.com

NetResults
1220 19th Street NW
Washington, DC 20036
Voice: (202) 466-8688
Fax: (202) 223-0566
E-mail: info@enews.com

NovX Systems Integration
316 Occidental Avenue South
Seattle, WA 98104
Voice: (800) 873-6689 or (206) 447-0800
Fax: (206) 447-9008
E-mail: info@novex.com
URL: http://www.interserv.com

Quadralay Corporation
8920 Business Park Drive
Austin, TX 78759
Voice: (512) 346-9199
E-mail: combs@quadralay.com
URL: http://www.quadralay.com/home.html

Studio X
1270 Calle de Comercio #3
Sante Fe, NM 87505
Voice: (505) 438-0505
Fax: (505) 438-1816
E-mail: webmaster@nets.com
URL: http://www.nets.com

❏ SERVICE PROVIDERS

The following is a listing of major service providers, many of which offer nationwide service. The largest service providers are PSI, NETCOM, AlterNet (UUNET), ANS, and InterServ (NovX). We worked with PSI, NET-COM, and AlterNet, as well as a local service provider, Portal Communications, throughout this project. You can also get a list of Internet service providers via e-mail called *The Public Dialup Internet Access List* (PDIAL), compiled by Peter Kaminski. To get this list, send e-mail containing the phrase *Send PDIAL* to *info-deli-server@netcom.com*. The InterNIC (Internet Network Information Center) also maintains and provides access to lists of Internet service providers. Call (800) 444-4345 for more information.

Services

Advanced Network Services (ANS)
1875 Campus Commons Drive, Suite 220
Reston, VA 22091
Voice: (800) 456-8287
Fax: (703) 758-7717
E-mail: info@ans.net

AlterNet
UUNET Technologies, Inc.
3110 Fairview Park Drive, Suite 570
Falls Church, VA 22042
Voice: (800) 488-6384 or (713) 204-8000
Fax: (703) 204-8001
E-mail: info@uunet.uu.net

BARRNET
Pine Hall, Room 115
Stanford University
Stanford, CA 94305
Voice: (415) 725-1790
Fax: (415) 723-0010
E-mail: info@nic.barrnet.net

Ccnet Communications
190 North Wiget Lane, Suite 291
Walnut Creek, CA 94598
Voice: (510) 988-0680
Fax: (510) 988-0689
E-mail: info@ccnet.com

CERFnet
California Education & Research Federation Network
P.O. Box 85608
San Diego, CA 92186-9784
Voice: (800) 876-2373 or (619) 455-3900
Fax: (619) 455-3990
E-mail: help@cerf.net

CICnet
2901 Hubbard Drive
Ann Arbor, MI 48105
Voice: (800) 947-4754 or (313) 998-6703
Fax: (313) 998-6105
E-mail: info@cic.net

Clark Internet Services, Inc.
10600 Route 108
Ellicott City, MD 21042
Voice: (800) 735-2258
Fax: (410) 730-9765
E-mail: info@clarknet

CNS Internet Express
1155 Kelly Johnson Boulevard, Suite 400
Colorado Springs, CO 80920

Voice: (800) 748-1200 or (719) 592-1240
Fax: (719) 592-1201
E-mail: info@cscns.com

Colorado Internet Cooperative Association
2525 Arapahoe Ave. Building E4
Boulder, CO 80302
Voice: (303) 443-3786
Fax: (303) 443-9718
E-mail: info@coop.net

CONCERT
P.O. Box 12889
3021 Cornwallis Road
Research Triangle Park, NC 27709
Voice: (919) 248-1404
Fax: (919) 248-1405
E-mail: info@concert.net

CRL
Box 326
Larkspur, CA 94977
Voice: (415) 381-2800
Fax: (415) 381-9578
E-mail: info@crl.com

CTS Network Services (CTSNET)
4444 Convoy Street, Suite 300
San Diego, CA 92111
Voice: (619) 637-3637
Fax: (619) 637-3630
E-mail: info@crash.cts.com

CyberGate, Inc.
662 South Military Trail
Deerfield Beach, FL 33442
Voice: (305) 428-4283
Fax: (305) 428-7977
E-mail: info@gate.net

Digital Express Group, Inc.
6006 Greenbelt Road, Suite 228
Greenbelt, MD 20770
Voice: (800) 969-9090 or (301) 220-2020
E-mail: info@digex.net

Engineering International, Inc.
2313 Headingly NW
Albuquerque, NM 87107
Voice: (505) 343-1060
Fax: (505) 243-1061

Global Enterprise Services
3 Independence Way
Princeton, NJ 08540
Voice: (800) 358-4437 or (609) 897-7300
Fax: (609) 897-7310
E-mail: info@jvnc.net

IDS World Network
3 Franklin Road
East Greenwich, RI 02818
Voice: (401) 884-7856
E-mail: sysadmin@ids.net

InterAccess
9400 West Foster Avenue, Suite 111
Chicago, IL 60656
Voice: (800) 967-1580 or (708) 671-0111
Fax: (708) 671-0113
E-mail: info@interaccess.com

Internet Direct, Inc.
1366 East Thomas #210
Phoenix, AZ 85014
Voice: (602) 274-0100
Fax: (602) 274-8518
E-mail: info@indirect.com

InterNex Information Services, Inc.
1050 Chestnut Street, Suite 202
Menlo Park, CA 94025
Voice: (415) 473-3060
Fax: (415) 773-3062
E-mail: info@internex.net

InterServ
NovX Systems Integration
316 Occidental Avenue South, Suite 406
Seattle, WA 98104
Voice: (800) 873-6689
Voice: (206) 447-0800
Fax: (206) 447-9008
E-mail: info@novex.com
URL: http://www.interserv.com

The Little Garden (TLG)
P.O. Box 410923
San Francisco, CA 94141
Voice: (415) 487-1902
E-mail: info@tlg.org

Merit Network/MichNet
2901 Hubbard Pod G
Ann Arbor, MI 48105
Voice: (313) 764-9430
Fax: (313) 747-3185
E-mail: info@merit.edu

MIDnet
201 North 8th Street, Suite 421
Lincoln, NE 68588
Voice: (402) 472-7600
Fax: (402) 472-0240
E-mail: nic@mid.net

MRNet
511 11th Avenue, Box 212 South
Minneapolis, MN 55415

Voice: (612) 342-2570
Fax: (612) 344-1716
E-mail: info@mr.net

MSEN, Inc.
628 Brooks Street
Ann Arbor, MI 48103
Voice: (313) 998-4562
Fax: (313) 998-4563
E-mail: info@msen.com

MV Communications, Inc.
P.O Box 4963
Manchester, NH 03108
Voice: (603) 429-2223
E-mail: info@mv.mv.com

NEARNET
BBN Technology Services, Inc.
10 Moulton Street
Cambridge, MA 02138
Voice: (800) 632-7638 or (617) 873-8730
Fax: (617) 873-5620
E-mail: nearnet-join@near.net

Neosoft
3408 Mangum Street
Houston, TX 77092
Voice: (713) 684-5969
Fax: (713) 684-5936
E-mail: info@neosoft.com
URL: http://www.neosoft.com

NETCOM On-Line Communications Services, Inc.
4000 Moorpark Avenue, Suite 209
San Jose, CA 95117
Voice: (800) 501-8659 or (408) 554-8649
Fax: (408) 241-9145
E-mail: info@netcom.com

NetIllinois
1840 Oak Avenue
Evanston, IL 60201
Voice: (708) 866-1825

Northwest Nexus, Inc.
P.O. Box 40597
Bellevue, WA 98015
Voice: (206) 455-3505
Fax: (206) 455-4672
E-mail: info@halcyon.com

NorthWestNet
15400 SE 30th Place, Suite 202
Bellevue, WA 98007
Voice: (206) 562-3000
Fax: (206) 562-3791

Nuance Network Services
904 Bob Wallace Avenue, Suite 119
Huntsville, AL 35801
Voice: (205) 533-4296
Fax: (205) 553-4296
E-mail: staff@nuance.com

OARnet
1224 Kinnear Road
Columbus, OH 43212
Voice: (614) 292-8100
Fax: (614) 292-7168
E-mail: nic@oar.net

Pathways
3220 Sacramento Street
San Francisco, CA 94115
Voice: (415) 929-4900
Fax: (415) 931-7931
E-mail: info@path.net

Performance Systems International, Inc. (PSI)

510 Huntmar Park Drive
Herndon, VA 12180
Voice: (800) 827-7482 or (703) 620-6551
Fax: (518) 283-8904
E-mail: info@psi.com

Phantom Access

1562 First Avenue, Suite 351
New York, NY 10028
Voice: (212) 989-2418
Fax: (212) 989-8648
E-mail: info@phantom.com

The Pipeline

150 Broadway
New York, NY 10038
Voice: (212) 267-3636
Fax: (212) 267-4280
E-mail: info@pipeline.com

Portal Communications Company

20863 Stevens Creek Boulevard, Suite 200
Cupertino, CA 95014
Voice: (408) 973-9111
Fax: (408) 725-1580
E-mail: info@portal.com

PREPnet

305 South Craig Street, 2nd Floor
Pittsburgh, PA 15213
Voice: (412) 268-7870
Fax: (412) 268-7875
E-mail: prepnet@cmu.edu

South Coast Computing Services, Inc.

1811 Bering, Suite 100
Houston, TX 77057
Voice: (713) 917-5000 or (800) 770-8971
Fax: (713) 917-5005
E-mail: info@sccsi.com

Spectrum Online Services, Inc.
2860 South Circle Drive, Suite 2202
Colorado Springs, CO 80906
Voice: (719) 576-6845
E-mail: jimw@sosi.com

SURAnet
8400 Baltimore Boulevard
College Park, MD 20740
Voice: (800) 787-2638 or (301) 982-4600
Fax: (301) 982-4605
E-mail: marketing@suranet.net

Systems Solutions
1254 Lorewood Grove Road
Middletown, DE 19709
Voice: (302) 378-1386
Fax: (302) 378-3871
E-mail: sharris@marlin.ssnet.com

Telerama Public Access Internet
P.O. Box 60024
Pittsburgh, PA 15211
Voice: (412) 481-3505
Fax: (412) 481-8568
E-mail: info@telerama.lm.com

Texas Metronet
860 Kinwest Parkway, Suite 179
Irving, TX 75063-3440
Voice: (214) 705-2900 or (817) 543-8756
Fax: (214) 401-2802
E-mail: info@metronet.com

Vnet Internet Access, Inc.
1206 Kenilworth Avenue
P.O. Box 31474
Charlotte, SC 28231
Voice: (704) 334-3282
E-mail: info@vnet.net

❏ INTERNET BUSINESS PUBLICATIONS

The following Internet periodicals are targeted at business readers. *Boardwatch Magazine, Internet World, ONLINE ACCESS,* and *Wired* are available on newsstands (or by subscription). The rest are specialized newsletters. We found *The Internet Letter* offered some of the best coverage of the Internet from a business perspective. The quality of newsletters varies, so ask for a sample copy of any newsletter before you subscribe.

Information Sources

Boardwatch Magazine
8500 West Bowles Avenue, Suite 210
Littleton, CO 80123
Voice: (800) 933-6083

Internet Business Advantage
P.O. Box 10488
Lancaster, PA 17605
Voice: (800) 638-1639
Fax: (717) 393-5752
E-mail: success@wentworth.com

Internet Business Journal
Strangelove Internet Enterprises, Inc.
208 Somerset Street East, Suite A
Ottawa, Ontario
Canada K1N 6V2
Voice: (613) 565-0982
Fax: (613) 569-4432

Internet Business Report
600 Community Drive
Manhasset, NY 11030
Voice: (516) 562-5000

The Internet Letter
Net Week Inc.
220 National Press Building
Washington, DC 20045

Voice: (202) 638-6020
Fax: (202) 638-6019
E-mail: netweek@access.digex.net

Internet World
Mecklermedia Corporation
11 Ferry Lane West
Westport, CT 06880
Voice: (800) 632-5537

Matrix News
Matrix Information and Directory Services
1106 Clayton Lane, Suite 500W
Austin, TX 78723
Voice: (512) 451-7602
Fax: (512) 452-0128

ONLINE ACCESS
900 North Franklin, Suite 310
Chicago, IL 60610
Voice: (312) 573-1700

Wired
544 Second Street
San Francisco, CA 94107
Voice: (800) 769-4733
Fax: (415) 904-0669
E-mail: info@wired.com
E-mail: subscriptions@wired.com
URL: http://www.wired.com

❏ WEB DESIGN SERVICES

The following multimedia design companies offer Web document and site design and production services.

Services

adfx-Virtual Advertising
E-mail: arnold3a@halcyon.com
URL: http://www.halcyon.com

Bonsai Software
2582 Old First Street
Livermore, CA 94550-3155
Voice: (510) 606-5701
Fax: (510) 606-5702
E-mail: ksedgwic@bonsai.com

e-magination
931 Maplecrest
Lancaster, TX 75146
Voice: (214) 227-7822
Fax: (214) 227-6628
E-mail: info@e-magination.com

Free Range Media, Inc.
316 Occidential, Suite 406
Seattle, WA 98104
Voice: (206) 340-9305
Fax: (206) 442-9004
E-mail: info@freerange.com

Michele~Shine media
1800 Market Street, Suite 204
San Francisco, CA 94103
Voice: (415) 621-0299
Fax: (415) 621-5023
E-mail: crmk@netcom.com

Young Ideas
207 2nd Street, Suite B
Sausalito, CA 94965
Voice: (415) 331-3128
Fax: (415) 331-9620
E-mail: indy@bonsai.com

❏ CONSULTANTS

The Virtual Contractor is a free online service that acts as a clearing house for businesses that need computer consultants. To access The Virtual Contractor, which is a Web site, point your Web browser to file://netcom2.netcom.com/pub/iceman/VC/VC.html.

❏ OTHER SERVICES

The following companies provide other services that are of interest to businesses.

Services

Aldea Communications, Inc.
7720 B El Camino Real, Box 117
Carlsbad, CA 92009
Voice: (619) 943-0101
Fax: (619) 943-0310
E-mail: info@aldea.com

Aldea publishes *NetPages*, a directory for the Internet modeled after the phone book—with blue pages for general information, white pages for individual and business e-mail addresses, and yellow pages for classified advertising for businesses using the Internet.

Internet Business Association (IBA)
655 Fifteenth Street, NW, Suite 200
Washington, D.C. 20005
Voice: (703) 779-1320
Fax: (703) 779-1362
E-mail: iba@intercon.com

The IBA is an organization founded to be a recognized source for public education about the Internet and to provide a voice for small to midsize companies that provide Internet services and products.

InterNIC
Voice: (800) 444-4345
Information services: (619) 455-4600

Registration services: (703) 742-4777
Directory services: (800) 862-0677 or (908) 668-6587
7AM-7PM EST (registration services)

InterNIC's mission is to provide information to individuals and businesses in a user-friendly manner. Funded by the National Science Foundation, InterNIC services are provided by three companies under contract: Network Solutions, AT&T, and General Atomics. Network Solutions provides the Internet registration services, including the assignment of IP addresses and registration of domain names. AT&T maintains lists of various types of servers available on the Internet, lists of white- and yellow-page directories, library catalogs, and data archives. AT&T also offers database design, management, and maintenance services to groups for material available to the Internet community. General Atomics provides a Network Reference Desk, the Info Source (a database of network reference materials), training classes and documentation for running NIS groups, and coordinating services.

Internet World Conference and Exposition
Mecklermedia
11 Ferry Lane West
Westport, CT 06880
Voice: (203) 226-6967
Fax: (203) 454-5840

Mecklermedia is the owner of a new trade show for companies providing Internet-related products and services for businesses and individuals.

Index